*I*ntimacies

Secrets of Love, Sex & Romance

by

Karen Kreps

Illustrated with photos of original sculpture by

Arye Shapiro

www.TrueIntimacies.com

Intimacies:
Secrets of Love, Sex & Romance

Net Ingenuity Publishing
Austin, TX

www.TrueIntimacies.com

ISBN 978-0-9797890-0-7

Special thanks to

Arye Shapiro,
my husband

Ken Martin and
Rebecca Melançon,
editor and publisher of
The Good Life magazine

Rebecca Price,
book designer

Sylvia and Sidney Kreps,
my parents

And all who have taught me about
love, sex, romance and relationships

$\mathscr{P}$reface

I was thumbing through *The Good Life,* a magazine about living an active and engaged life filled with enthusiasm, when I learned of the opportunity to write a monthly column about love, sex and romantic relationships. Years earlier, a literary agent had tried to coax me into writing autobiographically about being young, single and in the publishing world of New York City. At the time, long before *Sex in the City* was a television hit, I couldn't imagine doing anything so revealing about my personal life and feelings. I had dated scores of men and slept with a great number of them. Some of these relationships were deeply passionate, erotically compelling and unforgettably romantic. Too many, however, had been with men who on some level were unavailable, and my heart had been broken repeatedly.

Yet, after living in Austin, Texas, and being happily married for a decade, I knew in my heart that I could now write about how to be in a successful relationship and the intimate experiences of love.

I had writing samples from my earlier life as a magazine writer and editor, before I moved from working in print to early online media. My interview with editor Ken Martin went well and he selected me to take over the ongoing "Intimacies" column that had been published for more than four years.

Actually, I got more than I bargained for. When I applied, I hadn't realized that the job entailed more than taking over the column. It also required hosting an ongoing monthly public meeting that the magazine sponsored at BookPeople, the state's leading independent bookstore (named by *Publisher's Weekly* as Bookstore of the Year in 2005). The purpose of the group was to build community by bringing readers together to talk about "Intimacies" face-to-face. The Intimacies Conversation Group, which was promoted by both the magazine and the bookstore, usually attracted between twenty and forty people, singles and couples, first-timers and returnees, with a fairly even mix of men and women, ages eighteen to eighty. For each meeting, I would plan a topic and invite a special guest—such as a psychologist, marriage counselor or certified sex therapist—to lend expertise.

People came to ask questions, share advice and stories, and exchange laughter. For many of us, it provided a rare opportunity to talk honestly and openly with our peers about adult topics that are important.

Attendance was and still is free; audience members are asked only to come with an open mind and a sense of humor. While these meetings continue to occur in Austin, Texas, with the publication of this book and advances in Internet technology, you can now participate from wherever you are in similar discussions of love, sex and romance. Go online to www.TrueIntimacies.com and learn how.

What intrigued me about writing the column and hosting the group was having a platform and an excuse to address private behavior directly and openly. The keys I had been given opened doors to experiences I never would have imagined as hundreds, if not thousands, of people have shared their intimate secrets in these meetings and interviews for my columns.

Our romantic lives are normally kept so discreet that we rarely have a chance to talk about them with anyone besides our lovers—and some don't even do that. Instead, we operate in a vacuum.

There are many reasons for keeping our private lives private. It's not wise to kiss and tell. And extra-marital affairs or romantic liaisons in the workplace only invite trouble. Even within the context of a monogamous relationship, societal taboos and a sense of propriety about sexuality may prevent us from talking openly. Somehow, we assume we should have all our romantic affairs under control. Our ego wants us to give the impression that we know everything we need to about love.

Everyone wants love, yet it is challenging to be in a loving relationship, and people ought to be able to learn from one another about what works for some and what doesn't. That's the wisdom we share in the Intimacies Conversation Group meetings and that's what I'm sharing with you in this book.

Understanding emotions and managing feelings are the great challenges in life. I sought congruence between my inner world and the world in which I lived. I recall many family conversations in which I felt short-changed by superficiality. Rather than gabbing about inconsequential material matters, I longed for meaningful conversation about personal concerns.

I have become an advocate for giving voice to what needs to be said, even if it breaks a taboo or two. Talking and writing about the secrets of love, sex and romance is good for everyone. Sexuality is about expression and connection. Every facet of our lives is affected by our intimate behavior. Reducing stress, increasing vitality, being open to spirituality and having a positive outlook on life are benefits that come from sharing romance and enjoying sex, love's physical manifestation. Sex and romance are essential to our well-being and when these elements are missing our lives feel incomplete, wounded. At such times, we may want to pull back and avoid touching our particularly tender spots. But I believe that, with the right attitude, exploring those vulnerable spots is how we can best experience tenderness and enjoy our sensitivity.

Having this beat to cover gave me the unique opportunity to ask a lot of people, "So, how's your love life going?"

I am grateful to everyone who opened their lives and shared their experiences in relationship and the lessons they learned.

This book includes dozens of selected columns that I wrote between 2002 and 2007. These include personal essays, how-to advice, reports on trends, explorations of human behavior, and the accounts of many people who shared their real stories of love, sex and romance.

Each article is categorized by the subject matter it contains (love and romance, sex and sexuality, commitment, and money) and for whom it may be relevant (singles and couples).

It is my hope that men and women who are in special relation-ships with their lovers, as well as everyone else who wishes they had love in their lives, will use these stories as catalysts to spark conversation and experimentation. Take them to bed with you. Have fun.

"Seated Embracing Couple" (detail)
15.25" x 8" x 14.5," ceramic, acrylic, wax, 2004

Key to the Table of Contents

Topics explored in each column and for whom they may be relevant are indicated by icons.

Singles

Couples

Love & Romance

Commitment

Sex & Sensuality

$ Money

$\mathscr{C}$ontents

Part I

Part II

Part III

$\mathcal{P}$art I

1

Love will cool if Cupid's arrow finds the mark but once a year

After New Year's Eve, Valentine's Day was the holiday I most dreaded when I was single. For months in advance I'd worry about whether I'd have a date for the occasion. If I were lucky enough to have one, I'd expect so much from my boy friend *du jour* that he'd invariably disappoint me with his reticence about romance. If I didn't have a date, I usually lacked the emotional intelligence to show my lonely face in public. On New Year's Eve, everyone is entitled to celebrate the changing of the calendar year, but I felt that if you didn't have someone to be with on Valentine's Day, you'd be chopped liver.

Thank God that is behind me now. I've celebrated ten Valentine's Days with my Mr. Right and the holiday no longer provokes a personal crisis. It's simply an excuse for us to go a little gaga over our relationship and to express our love and lust. Still, if we go out for a special dinner, I sense our membership in an elite club of couples who flaunt red apparel in the finest restaurants in town.

Call it a Hallmark holiday, if you wish, but the day devoted to romantic love dates back much further than the greeting card industry. Valentine's Day probably originated from the ancient belief that birds, particularly lovebirds, began to mate on February 14. That was when the Feast of Lupercal was celebrated in honor of the Roman god of fertility. The same day also was once a Catholic feast day honoring a saint, a priest named Valentine, who, according to one of many legends surrounding the day, was beheaded for continuing to marry young couples after Roman Emperor Claudius II banned weddings. Apparently Claudius thought that married soldiers weren't as reliable as single soldiers. Through the centuries the various legends merged and Saint Valentine's Day became a day dedicated to lovers, a time to exchange sentimental cards and give flowers and chocolate as symbols of never-ending adoration.

So who needs romantic rituals? We all do, occasionally. Romantic rituals rekindle the sparks that originally ignited passion between lovers. They force us to pause in our mundane activities and to think about and express what our partners really mean in our lives.

The first few years my husband and I were together, a pre-Valentine's Day trip to Victoria's Secret was a no-brainer for my husband. I faced the bigger challenge of finding sexy jockey shorts in the men's departments of stores. I came home once to find a trail of paper hearts, stars and confetti leading upstairs to our bedroom. There I found gift-wrapped boxes festooned with red ribbons. Next came the fashion show. We would model our silky soft intimate apparel. It was never very long before our new clothes wound up on the floor.

As the Valentine's Days piled up, we looked for other rituals that meant more to us. We always exchange cards in which we write personal messages. Sometimes I get him to join me and watch the videotape of our wedding.

I surveyed a number of Austinites who told me about some of the special romantic activities they have shared with their true loves. They include sharing a bubble bath with aromatic salts, sensual foot massage or head massage; going together for massages from students in one of the local massage schools; surprising your special someone with a bouquet of flowers when least expected; watching the great violet crown of an Austin sunset; dirty dancing at the Broken Spoke; writing a love note; and saying how much your lover means to you.

These suggestions may seem trite, but whispering sweet nothings can result in significant rewards. Being romanced raises one's self-esteem. It stimulates sexual desire. Desire leads to fulfillment.

Remember the axiom, "Use it or lose it?" If you, as a couple, don't make time or mental space for expressions of love, you may become less able to express yourselves with each other in general.

You may begin to see your partner as a roommate, a parent, or a housekeeper. Do you go to bed at the same time as your mate? Do you take one another for granted?

Romantic rituals remind us of the private, soft connection we have with someone. If being romantic doesn't come naturally, practice a little. You'll be surprised at how easy it is and how much fun. Send a message that you find your mate special and worth spoiling. Affection breeds attachment. Attachment leads to commitment. Commitment offers security. That's something we all could use a whole lot of in this changing world.

It's not important to do something special just because it's February 14. But it is important for you to do something special *sometime,* and frequently.

Our romantic rituals aren't limited to annual holidays. My sweetie and I set aside Sunday nights for giving each other massage. And rarely is there a day when we come or go without a greeting kiss or a kiss good-bye.

Romance doesn't have to fade after its bright beginnings. As you mature with someone, you come to mean so much more to each other, and you find new, more personal ways to express your feelings. With hope, all romantic relationships will develop into mature love, but the sense of attraction, the racing pulse, and the depth of affection aren't ever really absent in a good relationship.

Whenever Cupid's arrow strikes, enjoy it!

Harmonizing two frequencies essential to good relationship

If your mind were a radio, you would have a wide selection of stations. If you are more visually oriented, think of your mind as a TV set. On dozens of channels, drama or comedy, news or music — something's always playing on your inner speakers.

Your mind may switch from one program to another. For a while a stream of thoughts may play in the background. Other times, you may be immobilized by certain ruminations and be so caught up in your internal drama that you forget everything else. You develop listener, or viewer, habits. Some mental broadcasts are heard in response to the varying events of your day. Yet others may contain themes, like soap operas, that have probably been playing all your life.

I have a couple of personal long-running programs to which I listen most often. One is a soap opera about an ongoing family feud, half a continent away. The other drama involves managing the business that pays my bills and getting my computer to work so that I can produce web sites that make my clients happy. There are other programs to which I pay attention, but those two are the main ones from which I find it hard to pull myself away.

We all listen to or watch these internal broadcasts. It is important for each of us to realize that other people may be tuned into their own broad selection of station programming.

Most people know that it is good telephone etiquette when you phone someone to ask if this is a good time for him or her to talk. Nothing like that happens, however, in face-to-face meetings. Sometimes I wish people would first find out if I have available bandwidth before they invade my reception area with their own noise.

Usually, when my husband comes home after being out all day, he's quick to talk about whatever he's seen or done since we were together last. I'm always happy when my sweetie comes home. I usually want to know how his day went and on what projects he has made progress. But sometimes his arrival disrupts whatever it was that I was focused on before he put his key in the latch.

He may be so wrapped up in playing his own program that I can no longer hear my own. If I don't turn mine off, or a least lower the volume, I am confronted with a cacophony of competing sounds. He'll come home eager to tell me about someone he met while walking downtown. Or he'll be all worked up about a local political matter. Or he'll want my opinion on whether or not to spend money renting a workspace he really wants.

Sometimes I enjoy temporarily putting aside my concerns and getting caught up in whatever my partner has on his mind. Other times, it feels like he and I are wrestling for possession of the remote control that selects which program we'll watch together that evening.

There are people who never get beyond themselves and their pre-occupations. I can spend an afternoon with some people and not once will they inquire about what has been happening in my universe. They are just too absorbed in their own world and worries: how to decorate their homes, rivalry with a coworker, getting their kid into college on a scholarship. I try to offer some news of my own, unsolicited, but with these self-centered people whatever I say seems to fall on deaf ears. I couldn't tolerate that kind of self-centered behavior in a marriage.

Whereas both my husband and I are articulate and inclined to communicate how we are feeling, I'm pretty passive in the race to dominate the conversation with my husband. I'll cede prime time dinner conversation and put my issues on a back burner until later on, when I trust they will be thoughtfully received. Sometimes that opportunity doesn't arrive until after I'm no longer listening to or interested in the program that was playing in my thoughts when my husband first returned home. When that happens, I try not to brood but to be direct and tell him that I never got the chance to share with him something that concerned me earlier in the evening. When I do that, he'll make a conscious effort to be more attentive—at least for a while.

It's wonderful to have a partner to whom you can reveal your inner dramas, your private recordings. Yet there will always be some programs that we must review alone, especially our reruns. My partner can only join me for a stroll down memory lane when those memories are based on shared experience. And each of us has some recordings that are ours alone.

I'll have flashbacks to places where I lived or traveled and about people I knew long before I met my partner. I'm sure he has similar experiences. Indications that my husband and I are tuned into different frequencies are not threatening to our relationship. They are simple reminders that we are separate individuals, influenced by events and memories that are uniquely our own. It is these emotional records that make us who we are. Knowing that someone we love may, at times, listen to the beat of a different drummer reminds us of our differences, and bridging that separation is what relationships are all about.

3

Is the elixir of love in food, or are aphrodisiacs hopeful hooey?

At a local art bazaar I recently met a vendor of fancy bonbons who did business in Austin as Sweet Venus Delights. Deep dark chocolate beckoned. I lunged for the last piece left on the sample tray. Was I in for a surprise! The rich bittersweet chocolate gave way in my mouth to a hot chili jam center.

The vendor was dressed in a chef's jacket embroidered with his name, "Chef Keem." The chef boasted that he had married the finest quality chocolate with a unique blend of natural strawberry jam, rum and chipotle chiles. "The combination of chocolate and chiles can be traced back to the great indigenous empires of South America," he said authoritatively. "The mixture accentuates the aphrodisiac properties of the ingredients."

Many of the delights he had on display came in the predictable shapes of Texas and armadillos. But others were erotic shapes. A pair of perfectly formed, white-chocolate breasts wore a lacy brassiere of fondant that could be removed to reveal breasts filled with sweet heat. I had a choice of orange, ginger and habanero; raspberry, peach and habanero; Cherries Jubilee and habanero; rum, pecan and jalapeno; or strawberry, rum, pecan and chipotle.

I hadn't given much prior thought to aphrodisiacs. These legendary love potions said to arouse passions and performance are named after Aphrodite, the Greek goddess of sexual love and beauty. Despite a five thousand-year tradition of pursuing sexual betterment through use of plants, drugs, and magic, the U.S. Food and Drug Administration dismisses the supposed sexual stimulants as bogus. Anyway, ground rhinoceros horn, Spanish fly, snake blood, and animal genitalia are just too gross for me to consider them a turn on.

The gentle burn that remained in my throat after the encounter with Sweet Venus Delights did, however, get me thinking about foods that seduce me. I love to eat good food. Certain dishes that stimulate my sense of taste, smell, touch, and sight also stimulate my libido. Some foods taste, well, like sex—especially the salty, creamy, melting kinds. At the top of my list is any kind of seafood, especially the pricey ones—raw oysters, lobster, caviar. Sometimes I want to lick the plate after saucing it up with hollandaise. Or chocolate sauce. Or hard sauce.

"Taste is associated with sexuality much more than Puritans would wish. Skin, bodily creases, and secretions have strong, defined tastes, as personal as odors," writes South American author Isabel Allende in her beautifully illustrated book, *Aphrodite: A Memoir of the Senses.*

In many cultures, fasting and abstinence are recommended for attaining illumination. To conquer the demons of the flesh, we are told to deny the senses. What, I wondered, would happen if I wanted to succumb to my senses? Was there a recipe for orgasm?

Love potions have been concocted from myriad foods that either resemble sexual organs or that pique the imagination with their aroma or texture. A romantic dinner can put you in the mood for love not only because of the intimacy created by candlelight and soft music, but because the vitamins and minerals in certain foods work with our body chemistry to lead to arousal and excitement. Spicy foods and caffeine have been viewed as aphrodisiacs because their physiological effects—a raised heart rate and, sometimes, sweating—are similar to the physical reactions experienced during sex. Some foods were glorified as aphrodisiacs based on their rarity and mystery. Most often cited for amorous potential are succulent fruits, chocolate, oysters, ginseng, pine nuts, eggs, and garlic.

Everyone's taste is different. Don't assume your lover lusts after the same flavors that you do. Experiment with each other. Eat slowly. Savor. Find those foods that contain the magic ingredients that provide peak sexual experiences that you both can share. Have fun experimenting with erotic edibles, and don't be afraid to play with your food.

On one of the many web sites devoted to the subject of aphrodisiacs, I found that a Swedish man had compiled a few basic rules to follow. First, the final preparation of a dish should only take a few minutes. Second, it should be satisfying without being heavy. Third, it should incorporate at least one ingredient with a reputation as an aphrodisiac. Fourth, it should give the impression of being more expensive than it really is. And, finally, the taste should be delicious and different.

There is one vegetable that my husband swears has, on more than one occasion, "saved our marriage." Before you get any ideas about me and my use of phallic root plants, I'll share the recipe with you:

Peel and steam parsnips and then blend with butter, cream (or milk), a pinch each of salt and nutmeg, and a few capfuls of Grand Marnier Triple Orange Liqueur.

Perhaps the ingredients matter less than the method. Preparing the favorite foods of my beloved is a way of showing love. It communicates my desire to please and to satiate. It reflects that I have paid attention to his personal likes and dislikes and gone to some length to purchase and prepare a dish especially for him. If all this creates the mood for romance, then so much the better.

"Female Torso (Elisabeth)" bas-relief,
11.75" x 14.5" x 2," ceramic, with rust patina, 2004

4

June bride pops the question: Why do we weep at a wedding?

I was a June bride. So was my mother. So were most of my married friends. If you attend a wedding this month or observe an anniversary, marriage and its meaning may be on your mind.

At a wedding the guests hope and pray that the couple will succeed in and enjoy a lasting marriage. We're a cheerleading team, rooting them on. They invite us to witness their nuptials and to hold that vision for them.

At a recent reception, between dinner and dessert, I left the dance floor to ask some guests about their responses to witnessing betrothal. Liquor had loosened lips by then and I found people happy to discuss why people weep at weddings.

"What makes me cry is the gravity of being involved in a ritual or sacrament so much bigger than any one person or couple," said Traci, a full-time mother of twins. "The reasons we cry are personal and depend on what relationship you have with the bride or groom. Marriage changes relationships, so you may grieve over losing a friend or son or daughter. Or you may feel relief for a friend who was lonely too long and you're glad to see their dreams fulfilled."

Once others at our table overheard this exchange, they listened carefully.

"I never cried at weddings until I wanted to get married, was getting married, or was already married," said Traci. "It's like having children, you don't really see other children as wonderful until you have your own and realize what hard work they are, and such miracles. Marriage is not just a way to get matching dishes. If you announce it to your community, arrange a party around it, and make vows in public, you want it to last."

A beautiful gal on my right chimed in. "A wedding stirs up a lot of thoughts and feelings," said Rasa. "Sometimes, I think about how many marriages end in divorce, but I still hope for the wedding couple that they succeed in their union and not have to go through that. I think about how important a vow is, 'until death do us part,' and what a challenge it is to keep. I always pray that my friends will make it. When it's a young couple, you realize that they just don't have any idea what it will be like and what they're getting into. If it's a second or third marriage, that's different.

"I divorced after many years of marriage. Now I regret it. If I had the skills and understanding back then that I now have, I could have worked through our problems. I now believe in lifelong partnership. We're here to learn and grow from each other in bad times as well as good."

While all of us were digesting Rasa's words, two women from another table, both named Rebecca, came by. After Traci revealed what we had been discussing, the Rebecca who was a graphic artist and a single mother gave her two cents.

"When we witness the parties at the altar, we make a quick comparison to our own lives. If we are happy, we feel happy with the couple. If we feel low on the romance scale, we then feel deep inner conflict or sadness about decisions we've made. At the time those decisions felt necessary, but we instinctively knew they that were robbing us of nuptial nirvana."

The other Rebecca, a singer-songwriter, offered, "I've cried at weddings after hearing readings express the love the newlyweds share. It makes me realize how alone I am as a single woman. I find myself going over what I do or don't like at weddings. I'll focus on what people are wearing, the bridesmaid dresses, flowers, music, and how the ceremony is staged. It's easier to focus on such things than on the emotions being stirred."

Most women in the group nodded in agreement. The two men at the table remained silent, hard to read. The singer continued. "I get a vibe from the wedding couple. I was in a wedding five years ago where the bride seemed numb; they divorced five years later. The wedding tonight is full of joy, reflecting the couple's sense of fun. I think this marriage will be full of joy. I certainly hope so."

The guys at the table had been too reserved, so I nailed one with a question about what he thought of all the wedding hoopla.

"I don't see the point of weddings," he asserted. "Just because you say you're going to be faithful in front of a group of people doesn't mean that's the way it's going to be. If a couple is true to one another, their behavior speaks for itself. If you want to have a big party, have a party—but don't go to all this formality on account of social convention."

The women were about to object, when I asked the other man, "Are you also so cynical about marriage?"

The man, who wanted to be known only by his initials, BNB, was there with his girlfriend of many years. "I get cynical when the people haven't known each other long and get married. They are so blinded by lust that they assume they are in love," he replied.

"Often, at weddings, people look at us as the couple that should be next. I'll know when the time is right. I love the way we can just be with one another, but sometimes I feel it's not complete because my girlfriend would love a ring and it would make her happy."

His partner laughed nervously, but BNB continued. "During the ceremony this afternoon, I thought about how beautiful my girlfriend looks and that maybe, one day, she will be the one up there at the altar, instead of whomever we're watching."

The announcement that the bride was about to cut the cake abruptly interrupted our group discussion. When the tiered white confection, topped with a plastic bride and groom, was cut, everyone cheered, and the bouquet was caught—by BNB's girlfriend.

5

Nature's paradox: Men want to love more than just one woman

"This morning I was talking to my girlfriend about some things I have learned in the two years we have lived together. I learned I easily fall in love with many women. I can't help it."

This intimate statement grabbed my attention and forced me to question my friend.

"Are you saying that you can love more than one person at the same time?" I asked Manny.

"Sure, my girlfriend is a beautiful person. Alicia rubs my back, she cooks me food, and she is a good friend and a fine roommate. She makes it clear how much she loves me. And I love her as well. But after two years, I am not as interested in her as I was at first. I see another woman and I can fall in love at first sight."

I asked what he meant by "fall in love."

"You know," he gestured from his chest, "your heart falls out and you can't stop thinking about someone. There's an instant attraction. You may call it 'infatuation.'" Then he questioned me.

"Don't you remember, back in high school, didn't you fall in love many times?"

Sure, I did. Over and over, and each love felt like the real thing, a greater love than the last. But doesn't everyone outgrow that?

"Not men," Manny insisted. "Most men never stop looking, never stop falling. That's why so many men cheat, or they go to one of the many topless bars that operate around here. It is natural for them to love more than one woman. In some other societies, like the Mormon or Muslim worlds, men are expected to have more than one wife."

I found Manny's politically incorrect dialogue outrageous. But after a little thought I had to concede. Historically, early in evolution, it may have furthered the species for males to have many mates. That way more babies could be born despite the mortality involved in childbirth. The women teamed up to take care of the home and children, leaving the man to go out and provide. But today monogamy is the social norm. In the United States and Western Europe, modern industry, science, and technology have freed women to do other work and men can be more involved in child rearing.

As if he read my thoughts, Manny offered his understanding of why monogamy is demanded in modern society. "Judeo-Christian religion tells us that adultery is unacceptable in the eyes of God. But that doesn't change the male inclination to be attracted to many women. That's man's burden.

"My buddy said that, if I have lost interest in my girlfriend and now only lust after other women," Manny continued, "and if I give up that lust, I might lose my desire for sex entirely. And I don't want to lose it."

"Some men can do that," Manny conceded, "but not most. Most men cheat or fantasize about being with someone else."

This conversation was making me feel particularly grateful for having a loyal, devoted husband. I was confident that he had no inclination toward infidelity. I flashed back to the long-ago hurt, shame, and rage I felt when a boy friend had cheated on me.

I told Manny, "I always thought that when a man divides his affection it is because he is afraid. It is a way for him to avoid a deeper intimacy. They do it out of fear of getting too close, of something beyond skin deep."

I asked Manny, "Don't you feel that you are enhancing the value of a relationship when you confine yourself to a single partner? You thoroughly invest yourself in it. But if you divide your love and energy, you are withdrawing from the relationship and diminishing its value."

"That's why I try to discipline myself," he replied. "If I meet a woman and my heart is drawn to her, I go home to Alicia and find that I don't feel the same way with my girlfriend as I was just feeling toward someone new. During my marriage of five years, I never cheated. Afterward, though, I made up for lost time with many women. And now Alicia and I live together, but it doesn't stop my eyes from wandering or my passion from flaring."

So what? I thought to myself. Everyone has his or her attractions. It doesn't mean that you have to act on every attraction. You could exercise some emotional intelligence instead. But I could see from Manny's expression that his conflict was genuine. And it was probably genuine for the majority of sexually active men. I've known some who clearly knew that their sexual drive was unusually strong.

Even as children, they felt a compelling attraction to women and they've always struggled with it.

"Doesn't your rapture with other women hurt Alicia?" I asked.

Manny shrugged. "I hope not. I don't want her to be hurt. But in my business as a musician, I meet lots of women. And my eyes will lock on one of them and that's that. I'm stricken. If Alicia comes to my concert on an evening when that happens, I will tell her that I've fallen in love with someone. I may even point out my new love or describe her. My girlfriend knows; at least I don't lie to her. Then we'll go home. The next day we'll wake up together and I will have forgotten about the other woman. She's no longer around. But Alicia is. And for that I am grateful. We share more than just physical love."

I began to understand that I had underestimated my friend. Monogamy was very difficult for him, and Manny would struggle with it all his life. But at least he was in touch with his real feelings, accepted them, and was able to express himself to his girlfriend with great honesty. Did he really need to tell Alicia when he was attracted to someone else? I thought not. But Manny seemed to have found a way of being so open about his sexual appetite that he and his girlfriend could both live in peace with it.

6

Money almost broke them up but love taught them to manage it

When Rachel and Dan married five years ago they enjoyed financial security, but rough times lay ahead.

She owned a house in Austin and worked part time as a physical therapist. Dan was well paid as a systems administrator and received rental income from two large houses, one near Dripping Springs, the other in north Austin.

Dan had always dreamed of living in a community. Co-housing intrigued him. "I wanted a residence filled with creative energy, a place of activity, not just a place to sleep," he said, "I wanted to live with thinking people willing to work things out with each other." Rachel shared his vision. She agreed to sell her house and invest in Dan's properties.

They opted to live in Dripping Springs, where ranches with many acres of wild cedar, mesquite, pecan, and oak trees bordered Dan's small property. The idea of living close to nature appealed to Rachel.

Dan had built the main house himself. It was complete and a second structure was under construction. "With ten thousand square feet we could have guests for week-long seminars," said Dan. They envisioned using the property as a conference or retreat center.

"At first, I didn't know how I'd make the place feel like mine. The kitchen was a dark hole in the wall, hardware was in every room," recalled Rachel.

They renovated the kitchen and installed a pool. She put in new carpets, tiled the bathrooms and planted trees. "I put over eighty thousand dollars into the property," she recalled.

It was the renters who drove them to sell the North Austin property. There, seven renters each paid three hundred dollars for a private bedroom, shared bathrooms and kitchen. "The place was a mess," said Rachel. "The wear and tear of so many people degraded the property. We lost money on the North Austin place, but I learned about ROI (return on investment). The way to win is to value our relationship over money."

When the rental market started dropping, Dan and Rachel were compelled to take in whoever showed up wanting a room. And they had a hard time collecting rents. "One renter was on disability, another was unemployed," recalled Rachel. "People were hanging on, barely making it." Rents would go unpaid for months.

"What bothered me most was seeing such waste and disorder," Rachel recalled. "I like things simple, neat. I came from a place where everything was in its place. My parents were simple Iowa farmers. Everything you ate, you grew yourself. In Dan's group houses there was too much stuff, too many computers, too many dirty dishes in the sink, too much fighting, too much slacking off.

You'd see people sitting around drinking beer in the morning. We suspected drugs were around."

When Dan fell behind in his taxes, mortgage and credit-card payments, Rachel begged him to sell the Austin property. One by one they got rid of the renters, paying some to vacate.

There should have been ten thousand dollars in their bank account after selling the north Austin house and paying off the debts. When a check bounced, Rachel discovered that the money was gone. She confronted Dan. "He had drained the account buying equipment and tools. I felt left out of the loop. Big Time.

"I packed my bags and took off. It was a miserable, rainy day. I drove toward Corpus. I needed to get away and think, write in my journal, and read. I had a copy of Wayne Dyer's *There's a Spiritual Solution to Every Problem.*"

After a day the weather cleared and so did the muddle in Rachel's mind. "Watching waves breaking on the beach, I realized I didn't need many material things. I got it all wrong. The problem wasn't Dan, but how I dealt with him: always whiney and paranoid. He wasn't good at managing money, but he wasn't evil. By the end of the day, I drove home and apologized for my reaction. That's when things really changed."

Dan told her that, while he had no sense of scarcity, he appreciated her awareness of their financial limitations. He proposed that he hand over all his money and leave the credit cards and fiscal management to her. They pared their expenses down to the essentials.

"It liberates me to have Rachel handle all the finances," said Dan. "We buy less and the bills get paid."

Rachel was able to get a full-time position with a health center. Before she could share her news, he announced that he had received a pink slip that morning. His office had switched technology and no longer required Dan's skills.

"I freaked at the news. *Oh my God!*" said Rachel. "But with my new salary and benefits, I'd be making as much money as Dan had made. Everything fit, even this layoff. Dan could get more grounded if he focused on finishing the conference center. I hired him to manage the construction and now I give him a weekly allowance. Dan contributes so much. He's always fixing things, doing things with energy, enthusiasm, and creativity."

Dan befriended an independent builder who was ready to work in exchange for living rent-free on the construction site. Dan got a single gal to pay rent and another couple, paying reduced rent, to help with the construction when they weren't at work. They formed the community he sought.

"We have a good life now," said Dan. "We're working out the money thing. Every day is a new challenge. And we appreciate how our differences really complement each other."

"You Wouldn't Understand" (detail)
female: 9" x 7.5" x 11.5," male:18" x 10.5" x 10.5"
ceramic, acrylic, wax, 2003

7

Being married doesn't mean that you and spouse are joined at the hip

Every June, when my wedding anniversary comes around, I think about what being married means. This year I have eleven years on which to reflect.

Although our wedding occurred long ago, it still has a strong effect. We made a life-long commitment. We packed as much ritual into the ceremony as we could, and our family and loved ones witnessed our vows. That was powerful juju. Our separate lives somehow got bonded together by choices we made and by ongoing choices that we continue to make. I don't think either of us has ever given a thought to ending the relationship.

We live together. We eat at least one meal together each day. We share a bed. We sometimes share a shower. We always kiss hello and goodbye. We update each other on the progress of our lives, the things we did, people we saw, conversations we had.

This doesn't mean that we always *like* being together. Over the years our criticism has sharpened and we tend to point out each other's failings and idiosyncrasies more quickly. His tolerance of my habit of leaving sticky fingerprints on everything doesn't improve any more than my tolerance of his visible nasal hair. But over the years, the bigger issues that once put us at odds have faded. We've come to understand that which we can change and to accept that which we cannot.

We share the household responsibilities—but how well we do that is a matter of opinion. Sometimes we squabble like school kids. When it gets too nasty, one of us will be sure to mimic the other until both of us have to burst out laughing. We've developed little "in jokes" and rituals that we repeat. For example, whenever one of us has been dogmatic about something that turns out to be entirely wrong, the argument isn't over until one of us says these four little magic lines: "You were right. I was wrong. I'm sorry. I love you."

Our lives intersect intermittently during the day, but the rest of the time we're very independent. He has his business, hobbies, and interests. I have mine. They don't overlap very much. That doesn't seem to bother either of us.

When a couple's goals and interests aren't aligned, it can be challenging to keep the relationship glued together. It's important not to get into a tug of war, to remember that you are on the same team. Sometimes one has to give way to the wishes of the other—though it's not always obvious who that one is.

It may take a little effort to show genuine interest in and support for our spouse's business affairs. We each expect the support of the other and, in order to not disappoint, we may have to patiently listen to the nitty-gritty details of an event or an issue that we'd just as soon not even think about.

I don't mind at all when my husband stays out late. I welcome the opportunity to be alone in the house. I play KUT FM, my favorite public radio station, in every room of the house. I open up all the blinds and enjoy the view from every window. When my husband's around, the radio is silent all day and, if I'm sitting at my desk, I'll listen to it with an earphone. Most of the blinds are drawn to filter out the sun's glare.

We make dates to be with each other: for dinner, for a day trip, for a swim. We'll go together to a party and spend the whole night talking to other people. But we know with whom we're going home and, as the old song says, "in whose arms we're gonna be."

My brother and his wife always took separate vacations. When I was single, I thought doing that was really weird. But now, sometimes, it just makes sense to go solo when it comes to visiting a relative or pursuing a passion that the other doesn't share. My husband and I like to travel together. Before we got engaged, we traveled together to England. We figured that if we could get through ten days on the road with each other, we could probably live together.

Because we circulate in separate venues, our friends sometimes never meet our better half. Most probably know we're married. They may hear stories about the mystery spouse. You wouldn't believe the number of times my husband has introduced me to someone and that person will blurt out, "Oh, hello. I've heard *all* about you!"

I wonder if some of my behavior may be unseemly for a married woman. I'll go on my own to hear live music and find myself talking to strangers at the bar. Or I'll go for a swim or take a walk with a friend without worrying about whether we're married. If a male gets too interested, I tell him that I'm happily married, and make a point to mention my husband in conversation every now and then.

There are some lucky couples that are able to really join their lives at home, work and play. Those relationships are rare. My parents are such a couple. My Mom ran my Dad's office for fifty-six years. Together they drove out to their mountain retreat every weekend. They never traveled without the other. Heck, they never took a walk without the other. I doubt as much as a day went by when they were beyond whistling distance.

Shortly before our wedding, my then-fiancé asked my father, "So, you and Karen's mother have been married now for over half a century. In all that time, did you ever think about getting a divorce?"

"Divorce?" My father laughed. "*Every* other day!"

8

Enjoy an afternoon dalliance even if you're happily married

Long before the sun rises, I'm usually awake and eager to jump out of bed, put on a swimsuit, and take myself out for a brisk swim in nearby Barton Springs Pool. I'm a morning person. But by the end of the day, I'm usually bushed, and I want nothing more than to curl up between clean sheets, read a few pages and then fall fast asleep.

My dear husband is more of a night owl. After dinner he usually gets a surge of energy. He is at his best—and most amorous—when I am likely to be cranky tired and not up for much of anything.

Do you think this creates a problem in our sex lives? Not really. Life and love entail many compromises. Sometimes one of us steps through the day's meridian in order to accommodate the drives of the other. But it only took a few months after we became intimately acquainted to discover that, for us, the best hour for meeting was sometime in the afternoon.

There's something about the afternoon that makes it special. Maybe it's tied to a taboo. Most respectable people are supposed to be busy working in the afternoon. Taking time out for a little hanky panky is a very deliberate act. It's not something everyone can get away with. We're fortunate. Both my husband and I are self-employed and so we are free to make our own schedules. Now we don't dillydally every afternoon. You can't run a business like that. But once in a while, when we find ourselves in the same room and have no pressing matters competing for our attention, we can indulge in a little libidinous behavior.

It happens spontaneously. We let the voice mail system take any calls that come in while we are both "in meetings." One of us may have to be pried away from his or her computer. Or we both may feel the need for a little siesta.

It's actually good for our businesses. A twenty-five year study by the Institute of Chronobiology in Marin County, California, reported that for ninety-two point five percent of workers, an afternoon nap increased their productivity and their creativity and problem solving skills.

The afternoon siesta is a tried and true convention in most Latin countries. Not long ago, unions in Greece went on strike when the cabinet proposed to abolish the three-hour afternoon break, during which workers go home, eat, sleep and relax.

But most of us think of an afternoon dalliance as something illicit that occurs, like in the movie, "The Postman Always Rings Twice," or "The Apartment." In the latter Jack Lemmon plays a clerk who curries favor with the executives in his office by giving them the key to his small apartment for the odd afternoon dalliance.

Though, sadly, sex in the afternoon often does involve adultery, it need not. I am friendly with a happily married couple both of whom work in executive positions for companies located at opposite ends of town. They occasionally exercise their non-exempt status to take long lunches. They'll say that they were going to work out at the gym, but they will rendezvous at a cheap motel off the Interstate midway between their offices. Once there, they work out a different kind of exercise regimen.

"There is something about meeting my wife in a tawdry locale and stealing off with her that we both find very exciting," recalls the husband. "We book a room for a couple of hours, and we sign in as Mr. And Mrs. Jones. I'll bet the desk clerk never imagines that we were really married. Sometimes we pretend to be having an affair. It's fun and it's safe at the same time."

Another friend, a single mother of two, tells me that the afternoon is the only time when she can arrange a rendezvous with her lover. "In the morning and evening the kids are around. I don't want to lock them out of my bedroom," says Cindy. "My sweetheart works the graveyard shift at a hospital. The afternoon is the one time when I can relax and let my hair down. I have been known to sneak an afternoon romp in the hay between chauffeuring the kids to soccer practice and picking them up after ballet lessons."

Her lover concurred. "It's different than making love to someone with whom you've spent the night sleeping naked in the same bed. That leads to a more organic kind of arousal. When Cindy welcomes me back from work wearing something she knows I find sexy, going to bed with her feels like something extra special, more an honor than an obligation."

In autumn, as the days grow shorter, you may observe something about the late afternoon light and the shadows it casts that leaves you feeling particularly romantic. The air is cooler and the warmth of another body gives extra comfort. Curl up under the blankets with your significant other. When you both return to the work-a-day world, you'll have an entirely different take on life. And only you and your partner will have any idea why you look so relaxed at the end of a long day.

Certainly it is lovely during any time of the year to enjoy an afternoon of intimacy. I will leave you with this quote from E.B. White, the author of twenty books of prose and poetry for children and adults:

"The first day of spring was once the time for taking the young virgins into the fields, there in dalliance to set an example in fertility for nature to follow. Now we just set the clocks an hour ahead and change the oil in the crankcase." — "Hot Weather," One Man's Meat, 1944.

9

Do not avoid the tender trap as it's a good place to get caught

Mother always tried to teach me, "Honey draws bees, vinegar repels them." The advice was usually delivered when I was being my most shrew-like. I didn't respond well to the dictum. I rejected it as antiquated wisdom, a by-product of my mother's pre-feminist upbringing. Both she and her mother had been ladies who knew how to humor a man.

But every now and then her words echo in my mind, and I've begun to think that mom was right.

Recall, if you can, the last time someone close to you did something special for you, something *really sweet*. And when was the last time *you* showered someone else with unexpected acts of kindness? However recent or distant, I'll bet it remains a pleasant memory. How did it make you feel at the time? And how did the subject of your affection respond to your generosity? A taste of honey made both of you feel great, didn't it?

Sharing the fruit of sweet action is the nectar that draws the bees and promotes the life of a species. It can signify intention in a budding romance. It can shine up a tired relationship. And it can lubricate our otherwise stress-filled lives.

The logic is simple. No one likes to be around a grouch or a grudge bearer, a worrier or a pessimist. Just because we live with someone doesn't mean that we should inflict our whining on that person. I'm not saying that you should be superficial or false or that you should never talk with your significant other about the hard issues of life. Sometimes it's okay to vent. I am only suggesting that you be mindful of how and when you complain, worry, nag or harp. Consider what it does for your relationship.

Compare that to when you present yourself in good humor. If you are cheerful, optimistic, and agreeable, how will you be received? Everyone with whom you come in contact will appreciate your lightness of being, but no one more so than your special someone, who will find you fun to be with and will crave your company.

Sometimes, it is just a matter of using a softer tone of voice and appealing to the other's sense of pride. Choose words that soothe and support. "It makes a difference if I ask my mate for things in a sweet, undemanding manner," reflected a friend. She told me that she gets much better results if she asks her boy friend, "Would you please help me with...?" instead of "Could you please help me with...?"

She said, "Men seem threatened or insulted if you ask, 'Can you...?' It's like you are implying that they are incapable of something."

Sweet expressions of affection come in all forms. It might involve bestowing a present—something of beauty or an item much desired by your beloved. It might be a gift of time. It may manifest itself as a physical expression of affection, perhaps even as a sexual favor.

It might involve giving an impromptu shoulder and neck rub as a special treat. It might be offering a hug whenever you greet or part from each other. It might be taking time out to talk to one another and to share what's deep in your heart. It might be a matter of noticing the other person's needs or acknowledging when your sweetie does something remarkable.

Actions speak louder than words. You can show your affection by taking some responsibility off the shoulders of your mate. Even mundane service can be endearing.

"You'll find clean socks in your drawer. I washed them this afternoon."

"I got the oil in your car changed after I took it to the car wash. You're set for another three thousand miles."

One of the best ways to show that you care is to take an active role in supporting your lover's particular aspiration. "My boy friend strikes me as irresistibly sweet when he demonstrates an interest in what I'm doing," a University of Texas music student told me. "He likes to hear me play guitar. He makes me practice and he never misses any of my recitals."

Tried and true expressions of caring, like bestowing flowers or preparing food, may be clichés, but they work.

One man told me he never brings home cut flowers, only fresh plants. He always installs the new plant wherever his wife wants it placed in their garden. She says she's surrounded by a garden of his gifts.

In our home, we often treat each other to gifts of food. I enjoy cooking a special meal. On occasion, my husband will come home armed with an elegant truffle. He knows that I appreciate the gift of dark chocolate, especially during that time of the month when my cravings are strongest. We'll sit down together and make a ritual of sharing it.

Is it mercenary to do something sweet for someone in the hope of buying a similar favor? Yes, it's mercenary. But it is also excusable. To care for and to be cared for is what most of us want. By taking a step in that direction, you encourage another to behave in kind. Kindness breeds kindness. Make love, not war. There are worse places to be than caught in such a tender trap.

As I write this, I worry that my words may come back to sting me. My husband will remind me of what I've written, should I be less than gentle in my interactions with him. He's apt to wrinkle his nose and note the acrid aroma of vinegar. But despite the risk of being challenged to follow my own advice, I encourage one and all to think about the countless ways in which you could possibly delight your true love. Do what you can to put a smile on that face you see when you wake up each morning.

"Alyssa" (detail)
12.75" x 9" x 11.25," ceramic, acrylic, wax, 2003

10

The holidays are inevitable, so make use of that mistletoe

Many couples report that holidays strain their relationships. They argue about spending too much money, or having to visit difficult relatives, or overeating and over imbibing. There's sometimes a tug-of-war over whose family takes priority, or over what to do on New Year's Eve.

It doesn't have to be like that. Instead of taking adversarial positions, turn it around in your mind. Team up with your partner to enjoy the holidays—or ignore them—in the best way you know. Gain more intimacy as you step through the final days of the year together. If you're lucky to be with the love of your life, you've already got the best present you could hope for. Remember: To your mate, *you are the gift.*

These ideas may help you stay merry. Use some of them and your children may just find mommy kissing Santa Claus underneath the Christmas tree.

Shopping—Strategize your holiday shopping. First, assess the importance of gift-giving with each other. Don't shop by rote. Make sure you each understand what—if anything—the other wants and if you can afford it. Think about whether the gift is being bestowed out of a sense of obligation or out of sincere generosity. The content of the gift doesn't have to be a surprise—you're too old to believe presents are delivered down a chimney.

After putting each other first, strategize whatever shopping for others is needed. Agree on a comfortable budget. Give the credit card to whoever gets the most jollies from shopping. The other one gets to pick up more responsibility on the home front: chauffeuring kids, cleaning up before company arrives, cooking holiday treats. If shopping is something you both want to do together, make the activity a pleasant event. Patronize interesting, independently owned local shops, rather than chain stores. You'll find easier parking, cheerful shopkeepers, and delightful, unique items.

Family—Whether relatives come to you or you visit them, you may have to deal with relatives you don't like or who may not approve of your choice of mate. Tuck it in. Remember, blood ties can't be broken. Hold your tongue for the sake of your sweetheart. Give your significant other time to visit with a rarely seen relative. Don't forget that you've both got an ally on whom you can depend for moral support. Allow each other to vent feelings privately. Find something in the situation or something about the person that you both can laugh about. Appreciate that, at least, you have each other.

The holidays usually throw us into close proximity with more relatives than we are used to seeing. Many couples alternate between families. The family not visited for Christmas gets visited for Thanksgiving. "At my husband's family I feel smothered, trapped," recounts Ann, a mother of a three-year-old girl. "It's because we are with them for days at a time. When we visit my family it's just a day trip. If family visits us, I do all the cooking and cleaning. It falls on me as the woman. Sometimes, I wish we could just stay home by ourselves and establish our own traditions."

Traditions—Establishing traditions that are your own is a wonderful way to build your nuclear family. Agree on which invitations to accept and which to pass up. Talk openly about the temptations to pig out. Indulge each other a little. Designate a sober driver. Find one or two things that you can enjoy together. Bake cookies and bring them to friends. Take the kids ice-skating. Watch a classic holiday movie. Attend midnight mass. Even if you are not a believer, it's interesting to watch others and you will enjoy the music. If you and your partner come from different ethnic backgrounds, demonstrate respect for each other by making plans for both of you to do something that stems from your diverse faiths. Host a holiday dinner for friends, especially those who are single or who don't have family nearby.

Volunteer together to do charitable service. "Last year my girlfriend and I joined a group of people who visited nursing homes on Christmas morning," recounts Alex, age twenty-five. "We sang carols and gave out small gifts that had been donated and wrapped during the weeks before. Some of the old folks really lit up when we visited with them; others were just too far gone. Neither of us had ever been in an old-age facility. It really opened our eyes. My girlfriend broke into tears as soon as we left. I think we're going to remember that Christmas for a long time."

Ignore the whole thing—"My husband and I stopped buying and giving presents to each other years ago. No Christmas presents, no birthday presents, no cards, no nothing," says Eddye, whose kids are in college and beyond. "We give to each other in other ways."

The best thing about this time of year, says Lynn, an artist, is that everything comes to a standstill between December 24 and January 2. "All our friends are away or busy. My husband's office is closed all week and we can do projects at home that we never get a chance to do at other times. Christmas morning is the best time to go downtown. There's no traffic on the streets. We bring our roller skates! The gift of the holidays is that Daniel and I have time together, quality time."

11

I'll hold you. You'll hold me. Take my hand, as one we'll be

Rarely thought about and almost never discussed, holding hands is one of the most meaningful and intimate forms of behavior in which we can engage.

Think about whose hand you have held. Notice the couples you see holding hands. They are young. They are old. They are passionately in love. Or they are simply dear to each other.

Children are often encouraged to hold hands, but once we're grown-up, we get to hold hands only with our partner, if we are lucky enough to have one—and if he or she likes to hold hands.

One friend lamented how a man she once dated wasn't into holding hands. At the movies, she'd feel the urge to reach over and take his hand. When she tried to do this, he would usually lift his hand up to rub his nose. That made the desire quickly leave her.

For most people, however, handholding can be an emotional or physical turn on. Call it old fashioned. Call it romantic. Holding hands can be a wonderful experience.

All of us have experienced the thrill—and wrestled with the embarrassment—of holding hands. We've all been through the first romantic, bashful experiences of touching the hand of another, when everything is new and we are just starting to make physical contact. It might happen at the movies, or in a car, or in the crowd at a local club.

"The incredibly wonderful way it feels to hold hands with someone you really like," a young woman testified, "only feels that way before you have had sex with him. Once you go all the way, holding hands changes. It's still nice, but it doesn't embody that thrill, that excitement. I think that when you're still pre-sleeping together, all your longing, desire—all the sexual feelings you have towards each other—is concentrated in the contact between the skin of your palms."

The hold itself comes in many variations. It is not static. The hands may squeeze and squeeze back. The fingers may entwine or they may roam. The senses may be tickled. The touch itself may feel warm, electric, thrilling.

A young woman described to her musician boy friend what it was like for her: "You've pressed my hand flat in your palm, and you're pressing my fingers like guitar strings. I can feel the calluses in your fingers, cylindrical and rough from fat classical guitar strings. I'm proud of myself for being able to keep up. The first note, your fingers in an arch over my pinkie, middle, and third fingers—D. Second note, first, middle, and pinkie—C. You press my hand into what might be an E, but might also be an A minor. I'm unsure."

How rarely do we touch anyone during the course of the day! Yet human contact, physical touch, is so important to our well being. Most of us crave the warmth of another, but fear of rejection inhibits us from giving in to those impulses. In almost all cultures, about the only part of another person's body that one may politely touch in public is the hand.

Yet some people feel very uncomfortable holding hands in public. One man explained, "Before you hold someone's hand in public you have to ask yourself: Is this person someone with whom I want to be seen in a PDA (Public Display of Affection)?"

Being seen holding hands in public is an achievement for some people, an affirmation. It makes a clear statement about their relationship, that it is intimate. It is a small, silent gesture that screams, "She's mine!" or "He's with me!"

The act of handholding certainly speaks volumes about the holders. It says that they have a physical connection. It makes it clear that they are not just casual acquaintances or business associates. It also reveals that each person has a tender side, a private life shared with someone else.

Historically, a suitor would seek a woman's hand in marriage. In romantic novels of yesteryear, if a young lady were seen holding hands with a gentleman caller, her reputation would be at stake if they did not wed soon after.

Today there remain backward parts of the country where a person, especially a man, could get beaten to death if seen holding the hand of someone of the same gender. Women can get away with it more easily. Gay teenagers say the thing to do these days is to come out at the mall by holding hands so all their friends can see. They get off on the thrill of liberation by behaving blatantly, regardless of what people think.

Handholding comes before kissing, or hugging, or any of the myriad sexual positions one may enjoy. And it can reoccur under the pillows as you fall asleep with the one you love.

A hand can say, "Let me protect you." Or "Help me up!" Or "Let's go now." Or "I'm scared." Or "Shhh! That's a secret." Or "I'm glad you're here." Or "Shall we make love later?"

There are many reasons for holding hands. It's called communication. It's what we human beings do. When we access each other's inner being, it provides the proof we all need that we're not alone in this world. These days, we can use all the reassurance we can get.

Touching a loved one's hand allows us to explore our differences, the unique qualities of each person. It is through this discovery that we experience beauty. If we see each other as more than reflections of ourselves, we experience each others' uniqueness. When we share our individuality, we share love.

When was the last time you held hands in public?

12

Have you got sex on the brain? Well, you're certainly not alone

Have you been thinking about sex today? You don't have to answer that, but chances are that the answer is: Yes, you have. Repeatedly.

The amount of time we humans spend thinking about sex is difficult to document. But it's safe to say that we think about sex a lot more than we admit. Not since "Don't ask, don't tell," became a military policy for homosexuals has there been such blatant hypocrisy.

The Judeo-Christian sense of guilt attached to sexual matters is behind our duplicity. Nothing touches us emotionally so much as sexuality; nothing so influences our lives. Yet, our sexual fantasies are rarely revealed, not even to our closest friends.

The attention we give to sex and sexuality has many variables: our age, our gender, whether we're getting any and, if we are, whether we're enjoying it.

According to research reported on the web by Mental Health Net, over half of all men think about sex once or more during the day, 20% of women do. Male college students have sexual thoughts over seven times a day, college women over four times a day. Over half of these thoughts are externally triggered. About 85% of men and 70% of women fantasize when they masturbate. And about 25% of us feel quite guilty about some of our sexual thoughts. These numbers seem low to me.

Anything on which you focus is magnified in your consciousness. Put thought toward something and you draw it into your life. Entertain sexual thoughts and you are sure to feel more sexually alive, more responsive, more attractive. Sexual thoughts help us to overcome sexual fears and provide a rehearsal for a real encounter.

The more you think about something, the more you want it and the less you are able to concentrate on other things. This is why coaches, teachers, and spiritual advisors sometimes discourage their charges from any kind of sexual activity, lest it detract from their athletic, academic, or devotional aspirations.

Taken to an extreme, fixation on sex can be an unhealthy addiction. If thoughts become obsessions that could influence your behavior, there is potential danger and you should seek treatment.

Keeping your mind off sex is hard, but finding stimulants for the libido is easy. A two-year study by Alexa Research, a web traffic measurement service, revealed that "sex" was the most popular search term. People want "sex" more than they want "games," "music," "travel," "jokes," "cars," "jobs," "weather," and "health" combined. "Porn" (along with "porno" and "pornography") was the fourth most popular search term. "Nude" (and "nudes"), "XXX," "Playboy" and "erotic stories" (and "erotica") were also among the top twenty.

"When men think about sex, they do so in a fairly innocent, harmless way," says my friend Hank. "Rarely do I find myself harboring explicit, porno-movie style thoughts about the woman standing next to me in the bus queue. I'm more likely to think, 'Mmm, nice bum,' invent a mental image of what it would look like in the flesh, and then return to reading my paper."

"As a single guy," Brian told me, 'instead of having to find a date, go out, and spend a lot of money—without any guarantee of scoring—it's easier for me to just stay home on a Saturday night. I've got a good collection of pornographic pictures and they provide good company with no risk of STD."

My girlfriend Katya told me about a sexual fantasy that I liked so much, I've started to have it myself. "I like to remember that everyone is a unique, human soul with the need for love and the ability to show love," she says. "So I look at a person's façade and try to envision what he or she might look like while being kissed or exchanging a squeeze with someone they love. I imagine them in orgasm. I picture their mouth, eyes, and their veins. I do this even with people I think of as ugly, and they become beautiful. People's personalities reveal themselves when I think of them: sweaty, yearning, delighted, glowing with passion, deeply engaged...."

Some daydreams are about actions one would like to experience, some are not. Most of us do not consider the thought as morally equivalent to the deed. Sexologists Masters, Johnson, and Kolodny write that having kinky sexual fantasies does *not* necessarily mean you want to actually engage in the same sexual acts (e.g. no one wants to be raped).

The researchers found that the common sexual fantasies of men and women are similar, except that women may imagine being in more romantic situations while men focus on body parts. Men are prone to imagine that they are doing something to the woman (dominating), while women imagine being done to (submitting). It is common for men and women to imagine doing something out of the ordinary or taboo, such as watching others having sex, forcing someone or being forced, receiving oral sex in a church. We like to imagine being desirable. We seek novelty. Especially during masturbation but also during intercourse, it is common to imagine having sex with someone other than our real life partner: a previous lover, a neighbor, a teacher, a celebrity, etc. (It may not be a good idea to disclose those fantasies.)

One thing's for sure, most of us spend a hell of a lot more time thinking about sex than having it.

"Woman on the Beach" (detail)
bas-relief, 11" x 10" x 0.75," ceramic, 2006

Part II

13

Master the fine art of cuddling through long, cold winter nights

What I like most about the month of December isn't the holidays; it's the cool weather that makes cuddling under the covers especially delectable.

Turn down the heater, crack the window for a bit of fresh air, and dive under the covers with your lover. Wrapped arms, entwined legs, warm hands, nuzzled necks, playful toes—what's not to enjoy?

While cuddling you can share warmth, explore the contours of your lover's body, deeply inhale each other's aromas and sample the flavors of love. Synchronize the rhythm of your breathing; sense the pulsation of each other's heart.

The great thing about cuddling is that is so relaxed. It's sex without pressure. There's no need to perform. You can take it easy. No effort is required.

Sexual intercourse is apt to be inspired more frequently when there is extended, affectionate physical contact than when sex partners retreat to opposite sides of the bed, like boxers returning to the corners of a ring between rounds. Should arousal occur, enjoy it. If not, enjoy it as well. Cuddling is more about expressing love and affection than it is about achieving orgasm. Call it the "slow sex movement."

The ancient eastern art of Tantra (which means "woven together") encourages slowing down and prolonging sexual activity. It was practiced originally in Tibet, China and India as a sacred act that unites the spirit with the flesh to achieve enlightenment. Tantra fans report that longer-lasting sex equals longer-lasting relationships.

Our bodies naturally crave physical contact. Fortunately, most of us had lots of physical contact as babies, but we wriggled out of it in the process of growing up and learning independence. Without cuddling and sex, the only physical contact most adults have is a handshake or an occasional brief hug. Our American society is not very touchy-feely.

Masters and Johnson, the team that followed the trail blazed by Alfred Kinsey in pioneering research in the field of human sexuality, reported that women not only need more time to become aroused and reach orgasm, but that they also need more time to come down from the peak of excitement. Afterplay is an often neglected area of sexual activity.

Look at singles ads. You can easily spot people—particularly women—who say they want "just to be with someone with whom I can cuddle."

By simply being together and holding each other without words, you may experience being loved, the knowledge of oneness, of belonging. In the right embrace you may share peace, fullness and joy.

Several adults who identified themselves as "good cuddlers" agreed to anonymously share their experiences with readers:

♥ "I like wrapping my arms around her and just holding her. So long as I can do that, I have the feeling that nothing is ever going to change as far as us being together, being safe and being comfortable. It helps me calm my mind and not brood over all the things that worry me like politics, my job, and the cost of living. When I can hold her quietly, it helps us set aside whatever we've had to deal with during the day. Hours may pass without conversation, but there is communication."

♥ "We'll spend the night in close physical contact. We're both light sleepers and we drift in and out of consciousness, into our own dreams, and then we may awake and again become aware of each other. I think a bond is reinforced by this, like a battery being recharged. When morning comes, she usually gets up before I do, and I always get a wake-up kiss—which isn't a bad way to start the day."

♥ "We usually both wind up on our backs, with his arm around me and my head on his shoulder. He'll let me know when his arm is growing numb, and he'll roll over on his side, facing away from me. So then I'll roll over onto my left side too, and get as close as I can. His buttocks fill my lap and we nest like spoons. I call it our 'fine sterling position.' After a while I'll start to feel the weight on my hip and so I'll turn over. He'll follow, and we'll just flip the position. This may happen two or three times during the night. When he is away traveling on business, I don't sleep as well as I do with him."

♥ "As a single person, I'm used to sleeping by myself, but I've been with men who roll over and turn away as well as men who won't stop touching me. I don't like either of those. One is too impersonal.

The other is too personal. I don't care for a guy who fidgets. What I like is when we feel comfortable enough with each other so we can lay still and just have a little contact. I like just holding hands, or maybe playing footsies. I can tell a lot about a man by how he lays around after we've had sex."

♥ "Cuddling is a great peace maker. We may have bickered or felt resentful about something one of us did or failed to do. But if we don't kiss good night and snuggle a little, it just feels weird. The need to touch magnifies our behavior toward each other and one of us always breaks the ice. It's like calling a truce and putting aside our differences for a while. We affirm that we are on the same team. Things always seem better in the morning."

14

Dive into the realm of the senses and, please, peel me a grape

Say the word "sensuality" and the first thing you may think of is sexuality. Yes, they are closely related—but should not be confused.

As sensual awareness deepens, so will sexual enjoyment. You can teach yourself to fine-tune the senses so that every part of your being is alert and alive. In the same way, you can also teach someone you love.

In daily life you may unconsciously filter our physical sensations out as unimportant. There are circumstances where conscious awareness of a lot of stimuli would be distracting and unwelcome. But if you explore your sensuality during appropriate moments you can allow passion and awe to enter everyday life.

To function appropriately in business and social interactions, we tend to split ourselves off from the impulses and energies of the body. For this we pay a very high price.

Most of our lives are overly sedentary, cerebral and focused externally. Spend too much time with your face glued to a computer screen and you can forget all about having a body—until it starts to give you pain. You are educated to use your intellect, not your senses. Focus entirely on the actions of others and you may forget about your own flesh and bones.

This disconnect has a large impact on the health and vibrancy of your body and your emotions. It unplugs you from the circuitry of your nervous system that shows you are alive. When it comes time for romance, it isn't easy to switch gears and feel the thrill of Cupid's arrow.

Happily, you can rectify that imbalance. You'll find it easy to dive into the realm of the senses. All it takes is a conscious decision to pay close attention to what you smell, taste, touch, hear and see. No special equipment is needed, no particular time and no one's cooperation—though having a partner makes it much more fun!

You can train your body to run, swim, or lift weights. You can also train your body to experience and sustain pleasure through the senses. Instead of undertaking an endurance exercise, practice an exercise in delight.

In the right state of mind almost anything can be a sensual experience: waking to the song of birds, selecting clothing to wear, sipping coffee, making the bed, smelling fresh laundry, singing along with the radio.

Sensual exploration isn't necessarily an indoor sport. Lift your face to the sun. Feel the breeze and watch the patterns of light under your closed eyelids. Take a hot sauna and then jump into some icy water. Lie down on the grass and inhale the scent of earth. Listen to the ambient sounds of the world in which you live.

Tactile epiphany is not limited to soft, smooth, satin sensations. It may even be a little rough or uncomfortable. It might be prickly—like the stubble on his cheek or on her legs.

Sensory awareness does not mean sensory overload. Turn off the lights or put on a blindfold and your sense of touch, smell and sound will be keener. Subtle nuances become very large events. Less can be more.

I once took a "Sensory Awareness" class at the Naropa Institute in Boulder, Colorado. I signed up thinking it might be some kind of group grope. It was nothing like that. Each week, we lay comfortably on our backs for ninety minutes while the instructor, Ben Weaver, guided us through extremely detailed inventories of our anatomies. It took five classes to cover the entire body. I experienced bodily tissues and pulsations I had not known about. At the end, I felt like a completely new person. I felt more present in the here and now. When I walked, my whole body was engaged, not just my legs. I breathed more fully. Food tasted better. I felt reconnected with life.

Sharing food is a popular way to stimulate the senses. "Ever since Marc Anthony first fed Cleopatra grapes, sensual foods have been intertwined with romance," author Martha Hopkins, states in *InterCourses: an aphrodisiac cookbook*. In addition to recipes conceived to stimulate more than your appetite, the book features stunning photographs of food arranged on beautiful naked bodies.

"We usually take food for granted and don't think much about what we are eating," says Hopkins. "With aphrodisiacs you slow down and appreciate all that food has to offer.

"Food isn't just for the palate. It may involve all the senses. The appearance and the aroma can be as pleasing as is the taste. Aphrodisiacs are foods that stimulate all the senses. Honey, for example, is golden, sweet and sticky. It has smell, taste and texture that you can sense on the tongue and as it goes down."

Explore the texture of fresh foods: melons, peaches, avocados, asparagus. Play with your food. It doesn't have to only go in your mouth.

When your senses are fine-tuned, you may find that you become more alert and aware of subtle things. You may be more sensitive to other people. You may even begin to experience a sixth sense, a form of intuition. Pay close attention to any messages that you may receive telepathically. You may feel closer to those you love and your relationships may become even more meaningful.

You can safely indulge in sensuality by yourself in secret—but sensuality is contagious. Share yours openly and your loved ones will be more aware of and enjoy their own sensuality.

15

A romance of over six decades deserves a daughter's homage

I can't get past June, a month that includes Father's Day and two significant anniversaries, without sharing some of the story of my parents' remarkably stable marriage.

My folks were part of what Tom Brokaw calls "The Greatest Generation." Raised during the Great Depression, they survived World War II and made sacrifices to create a better life for their two children.

They met at a picnic, introduced by friends. She waited seven years for him to complete training to become a doctor. Each was truly the other's one-and-only love. My parents presented a rock-solid unit throughout my adolescence in the nineteen-sixties, while the national divorce rate shot upward. "Our family doesn't divorce," my father would boast.

My brother's response to that assertion was to hang onto his marriage despite its normal challenges. My response was to delay marrying until it was almost too late.

For fifty-six years our parents ran a mom-and-pop business. He practiced medicine. She ran the office. My mother gave up a career teaching English to take a permanent position as partner in Dr. and Mrs. Sidney I. Kreps. The job involved being office manager, receptionist, bookkeeper, insurance expert, and patient representative, not to mention social secretary and chief cook and bottle washer.

He was the figurehead in the family; she was the invisible force behind him. I'd learn later about the Hindu concept of Shiva (the manifestation) and Shakti (the power). That was them.

I think that they must have had great sex lives. They were affectionate—but they were quick to close the bedroom door when it was time for the grownups to be alone.

They were romantic. I remember my parents telling me that we should put them on an ice floe and send them down the river when they became old and burdensome. It didn't matter, said my mother, so long as they were together. (I reminded them of this when I started to find them old and burdensome but, by then, they denied having said anything of the kind.)

The two were together for almost everything: office hours, meals, gardening. Whenever my father took on any kind of project, my mother would be on call, as a ready assistant. When he'd repair something around the house, she'd hand him nails as he hammered them. Except when she was in the hospital giving birth, they never spent a night apart from each other. My father rarely did so much as take a walk without my mother. Usually they could be found no more than fifty yards apart.

They talked to each other about everything. After many years, the communication became intuitive and involved fewer spoken words.

My father assumed his responsibilities as the head of the household and gift to modern Western medicine with dignity and dedication. She bore her responsibilities selflessly and with a sense of humor. They both were respected by their friends, neighbors, and the people they served. They both took active roles in their children's education. Mom deferred to dad's authority, while maintaining clear command of their domestic life.

In their generation, men of means never did dishes. They never even cleared the table. Occasionally my mother would confide in me that she wished that the boys would do more of the housework, but she never expected that of them. She was happy with what life had presented to her.

When we were young, she worked like a slave, sometimes with domestic help, usually without: putting on formal dinner parties for my father's colleagues and their wives; cooking, cleaning, shopping.

After the kids were grown, and the economy was strong, they could afford to travel and they visited all five continents. Each vacation, they said, was like a honeymoon for them. They enjoyed fine dining, fine clothes and top entertainment. They had only positive, loving things to say about each other. My father often complimented her to their friends. He wanted her to buy the best things.

Sadly, all the money in the world couldn't stop the onset of Alzheimer's disease. It gradually robbed us all of my mother's bright intellect. Then it robbed us of most of what was left of her mind.

My father might have kept working forever, but my mother needed someone to look after her. No one else could do the job as well as her husband, the doctor. He closed his practice, not only because she needed to be watched closely, but because he just didn't want to be apart from her all day.

At an age when most men might themselves be in nursing homes, he learned to manage tasks he'd never had to do before: cooking, cleaning, and writing checks. We begged him to accept some hired home care, but he refused. The intrusion of a stranger into their private world was something he would not tolerate until he absolutely had to.

I'm sure that it is love for each other that keeps them alive day by day. In June 2004, my husband and I will have celebrated our twelfth wedding anniversary. One day before that, God willing, my parents will have celebrated their sixty-third. Different as our lives may be, there's still a lot to be learned from them.

"Water Bearer"(detail) bas-relief,
25.5" x 13.75" x 1.125," glazed ceramic, 2007

16

Ask, 'Is sexual chemistry real?' and you've yet to experience it

When sexual chemistry exists, you can't help but notice. You have felt your blood stirred merely by the physical proximity of a particular person. It may hit you without warning. You'll feel a welling of desire, a flush of excitement, a private moistening. It may occur with the love of your life or with a stranger. It even may occur with someone you've known for a long time but never saw in a particular light—until you felt aroused.

When people talk about whether chemistry is "real," they're usually talking about whether it is shared. The chemical reaction may occur only between a single set of ears and will eventually fizzle, but *if it is reciprocal,* the reaction can lead to combustion.

Sexual chemistry is best enjoyed firsthand but is frequently observed vicariously. Millions of us enjoyed watching the sexual chemistry between movie stars Bruce Willis and Cybill Shepherd in the television series *Moonlighting,* which aired in the late nineteen-eighties. We could see it in how the two looked at each other, in their body language and in the way they reacted to each other.

Sexual chemistry may be experienced on an unspoken level between two people, even before any relationship is formed. Likewise, it is a measure of how compatible people will be when they actually have sex.

When you are sexually aroused, chemical changes take place in your brain and affect your body, your behavior and your feelings. An idealization of the love object may lead to errors in judgment.

Researchers from the University of Connecticut and Elon University in North Carolina found that, after a brief five-minute first meeting, men were more likely than women to experience sexual chemistry when the feeling wasn't mutual.

What are the biochemical processes underlying such mysterious emotions such as attraction, passion and love?

They mostly involve hormones, chemical messengers that tell organs in the body what to do. The word "hormone" comes from a Greek word meaning "set in motion."

Researchers from the University of Pisa in Italy tested the levels of hormones in the blood of volunteers who were rated on a passionate love scale. Levels of these chemical messengers were much higher during the early stages of romance, but in twelve to twenty-four months these so-called "love molecules" were greatly reduced and replaced by oxytocin, the "cuddle hormone." (Oxytocin is a hormone that induces labor, aids uterine contraction during birth, and is released during sexual orgasm by both men and women.)

Similar research from the University of Pavia in Italy found that levels of a chemical messenger called nerve growth factor (NGF) increased with romantic intensity. After a year or two, NGF levels returned to normal.

A woman has a cyclical production of sex hormones and is more apt to be aroused before ovulation, about two weeks before her period; a man's level of sex steroids stays pretty constant.

Testosterone increased in love-struck women, but was reduced in men when they were in love. Maybe falling in love reduces some of the differences between the sexes, softening men and making women more aggressive.

Pheromones are subtle scent chemicals produced by an organism that attract members of the same species. In insects, pheromones can attract males to their deaths. We humans, however, are trained to think that body odors are nasty. A whole industry is devoted to ways of making you smell better. Bad personal odors may drive us away, but usually we are only subliminally aware of them. We tend to be attracted to people who smell different than we do. This ensures diversity and strengthens the species.

We humans have long sought a magic elixir that can help provoke a sexual response. Gayle Engels, education director of the American Botanical Council (www.herbalgram.org), says that certain plant materials are believed to have an influence on human sexuality.

Damiana, she says, has been used as an anti-depressant and to treat inorgasmia in women. It is a pretty green shrub with little five-petal yellow flowers that grows in the American Southwest. The leaves have been dried and smoked or used as an infusion but an alcoholic decoction is recommended.

"There's been little or no clinical study of these traditional claims," says Engels. "But in 1998 in a small, month-long study published in the *Journal of Sex and Marital Therapy*, ginkgo biloba was studied and found to be eighty-four percent successful in treating sexual dysfunction caused by certain antidepressant medication." Women were more responsive than men (ninety-one percent vs. seventy-six percent). The study concluded that ginkgo could have a positive effect on desire, excitement, orgasm and the resolution phases.

Some aphrodisiacs are said to increase sperm count, but most stimulate digestive juices. These include all the capsicums and spices such as garlic, coriander, cardamom, anise, and gotu kola. "If you're flatulent, you won't be a happy candidate for coitus. The best aphrodisiac," says Engels, "is good health and the right attitude."

17

Ambiguous and potentially risky, but flirtation has its rewards

There are a lot of worse things you could be told than that you are a flirt. Flirting and feeling happy go hand in hand. Flirting is good for the psyche and the libido.

What does it take? Playfulness, humor and charm.

You can flirt with your beloved, with a stranger or with a friend. Everyone can do it, young and old, single or not so.

Your ability to flirt says that you feel confident about yourself and your sexuality. You've relaxed enough to make light of it.

I know two happily married couples who take turns hosting each other for dinner. After every splendid meal, the visitor will say to the cook, "That was great! Will you marry me?"

That's a harmless flirtation. Flattery is always welcome, for everyone likes to be acknowledged and appreciated. In return for your compliment, you will be appreciated for noticing the positive and being open enough to voice it. Flirt with respect and it will usually be well-received. Be alert to the response you get and back off unless you're encouraged.

All it takes to flirt is making eye contact and smiling. A wink, a lift of the eyebrow, a lick of the lips, a coy toss of the head—body language conveys the flirtation. Assume an inviting posture. Take your hands out of your pockets.

It doesn't matter so much what you talk about—though you'll get a better response if you ask engaging questions about the other person rather than focusing on yourself. All flirtation basically communicates the same thing: that the two of you are human, sexual and able to relate in a personal way.

Janet Trent Morehead is a dating coach who teaches how to "Ignite Your Mojo—Discover Your Personal Magnetism" through the University of Texas Informal Classes. She says, "People who come to my class are afraid to make eye contact. Some have stories they've made up about why they can't flirt. I help them quiet all that mind chatter. They lack self confidence and I coach them with their image styling. I teach them to identify their own personal brand, what makes them fun to be with. They learn to promote that brand.

"What makes people attractive is that they have enough self confidence to be with others," says Morehead. "When someone feels you are really *with them*, they want to be with you."

Flirtation patterns fluctuate geographically. Many Asians were raised to think it rude to look directly at someone, so making eye contact may be difficult for them. Popular wisdom asserts that women who were raised in the South are more flirtatious than those from colder climes. My friend Gloria remembers that when she got married and moved north to New York City her husband discouraged her from smiling at strangers on the street. "They'll think you want to pick them up," he told her.

How you play with flirtation all depends on what you want from it. You may be seriously looking for a mate or just polishing your shine. You can flirt with serious innuendo or harmless banter.

Lisa flirts under the table. In a restaurant she removes her sandals and rubs her toes against her sweetie's ankle and calf. Doing this, she says, sends a personal signal that will arouse interest and subsequent action.

In contrast, Lynne has flirted casually with one man for five years. "We do it on the dance floor. We make all kinds of provocative moves and have fun knowing that, because we're both married, it's never going to go further. It's safe."

Some people believe that they don't have it in them to flirt. Renee is one. She's single and attractive and has a good sense of humor. She tells me that she is afraid to flirt. "I'm very shy. If I flirt with a guy, he's going to think I want to go to bed with him. I don't want to lead him on or encourage him."

In her blog on www.intimatewisdom.com, Gayle Michaels, an Austin-based certified sexologist, addresses this problem. "Women who have the courage to simply flirt deserve to be saluted in this society. They are frontline sexual healers. If men want women to become more relaxed in bed, they need to lighten up when women flirt. Don't presume flirtation is an invitation to have sex. If you get rejected by a flirtacious woman, don't get all embarrassed or angry and try to ruin her reputation to save face. Lusty innuendos, especially in public, will turn her off and make her wish she hadn't flirted."

Ritchie grew up in New York. He said that when he got his own place at age twenty-two, it was the perfect time for him to flirt with women—but he refrained because he didn't want to offend any feminists. "That restraint got me *nowhere!*" he recalled ruefully.

Another buddy told me he'll always remember his friend's kid brother, who behaved just the opposite way. "No matter where he'd go, whenever this guy would meet a woman, young or old, beautiful or plain, he'd give her a big wink. I couldn't figure out what was going on until his brother explained to me, 'He thinks it's a numbers game. If he flirts with enough women, some of them will respond positively.'"

Today, flirting is a socially permitted form of naughty behavior. Austin-based sexologist and intimacy coach Charla Hathaway asks, "Why were we taught that flirtation was bad? Why weren't we taught that our role is to *attract* and that that's our job? How else would this world turn around?"

18

Forget all of your old excuses, put a priority on your pleasure

We come up with all kinds of excuses for not having sex. There's no time. We're too tired. I'm just not interested. There's too much work to do. We can't with the kids around. There's no privacy now that Mom is living us. I'm grumpy. I'm too old for that. My back hurts. I've got worries. My partner really doesn't want it as much as I do. It's too hot and humid. I just want to veg out after a hard day at work. She's morose. I'm still ticked off. I just want to finish my book. My partner didn't give me the support I asked for, so I'll teach him a lesson. She's put on weight and I prefer looking at adult models on the web.

Sex is one of the most common and, certainly, most pleasurable, activities we humans experience. After a while, though, many of us lose interest in cohabitating or sex or fail to prioritize it in our lives. There's good reason to reevaluate your behavior and prioritize having sexual pleasure.

Unused, a man's testicles shrink and the gonads drop. He gets horny and, because he becomes more easily aroused and quick to climax, he loses sensitivity and skill as a lover. In contrast, the less often a woman has sex, the less she will want or enjoy it. The walls of the vagina secrete less. It may become difficult to become aroused and experience orgasm.

Having frequent sexual relations, on the other hand, has a lot of very positive outcomes.

It's a great workout. During sex heart rates can rise as high as those in vigorous aerobics. The act of intercourse burns about 200 calories, the equivalent of running for 30 minutes. Contractions during intercourse work muscles in the pelvis, thighs, buttocks, arms, neck and chest. Regular sessions firm not only belly and buttocks but also improve posture. *Men's Health* magazine has called the bed the single greatest piece of exercise equipment ever invented.

In addition to physical health rewards (longevity, reduced rates of heart disease and cancer, enhanced immunity, pain reduction and greater regularity of sleep and menstrual cycles), sexual pleasure offers psychological, emotional and social benefits.

A survey of nearly thirty-five hundred adult Americans showed that personal happiness is associated with the frequency of sexual activity and orgasm—especially among women. With more of it, everyone involved will look better: rosier, more relaxed, happier. Your relationship will be more vibrant. You'll have something to which you can look forward.

Studies have shown that the surge of the hormone oxytocin, which occurs during orgasm, stimulates feelings of affection, intimacy and closeness with a sex partner. Statistics correlate sexual satisfaction to the stability of relationships. If you know that your partner finds you attractive and wants to give you pleasure, your self-confidence will be enhanced and you will be able to perform better in bed.

"Just as your body needs nutrients to stay healthy, your relationship needs sex to stay strong," writes best-selling author Laura Corn in her book, *The Great American Sex Diet*.

She warns, "Most of us think that we have to feel close in order to have sex, without realizing that having sex makes you feel close."

Start by talking with your partner about why you think it's a good idea to step up the pleasure factor. This conversation should take place outside of the bedroom in a neutral environment. Refrain from whining or taking any nasty digs at the other person. Listen carefully to how your partner feels. No one should feel pressured or coerced. If you ask, real nice, you probably will get a positive response. Just hearing the request may serve as a stimulant.

One of you may feel a greater need to make excuses than the other. Still, with a little friendly negotiating, you can identify common goals: to help each other get more in touch with your sexuality and, especially, to have fun.

To achieve that you can try all sorts of things. To avoid boredom, try variety. Shake it up a little with new positions and new locations. Try out something that you read in a book or imagined doing. Curl up together in front of the DVD player to watch an erotic movie. Take risks. Surprise yourselves by altering your schedule. Weekends aren't the only time for romance. If you're too tired after a hard commute, do it before dinner. Everything will taste better.

Support each other in your pleasure pact and come up with a plan of action. Review this plan periodically. Resolve to interact in a way that can be measured.

Set dates to which you can look forward. Send each other naughty reminders of what is to come. The anticipation is half the fun.

Putting pleasure first requires some ingenuity. Cultivate friends and family members who will take the children off your hands. Or arrange sleepover dates. Take a vacation together, or, if you can't swing that, stock up on delectable food, unplug the phone for the weekend and disappear into your own private pleasure palace.

The world won't go away just because you are getting it on more, but the stressors in your relationship may be easier to handle. You must simply draw a truce when you share physical and emotional intimacy. It's hard to remain irritated with someone you've just been kissing.

Drop those excuses, prioritize pleasure and you'll bask in the afterglow.

"Steph I" (detail) bas-relief,
16.5" x 11.75" x 0.625," ceramic, acrylic, wax, 2004

19

Sweet are the memories of the lips that first kissed ours

Put your lips together, pucker and press. A kiss is one of the most sensuous ways to express love or affection. It is something that you cannot give without taking and cannot take without giving. Kissing can be an enjoyable prelude to more intimate pleasures or a joy unto itself.

In her book, *Anatomy of Love: The Natural History of Monogamy, Adultery and Divorce,* Helen Fisher, PhD, of Rutgers University, reported that, worldwide, ninety percent of people practice some form of kissing.

Like the word *aloha,* a kiss is used in both greeting and parting. It bridges language and culture. It's a sign of peace. It is an instrument of healing. You kiss a boo-boo so it feels better.

The ancient Romans assigned words for different types of kisses. *Osculum* means a kiss of friendship. *Basium* means a kiss of passion. *Savium* means a deep kiss, otherwise known as the French kiss.

In fairy tales, a well-timed kiss could wake Sleeping Beauty from prolonged coma and turn a frog into a prince.

The chaste, nurturing kisses between parent and child build lifelong trust. We may have kissed a brother or sister. We were taught that we should "kiss and make up."

In social situations, we often greet one another with air-kisses. Such close encounters throw us into proximity beyond our normal boundaries. They occur fleetingly—embracing the arms or shoulders, touching cheek to cheek and blowing a kiss somewhere beyond the ear. It's cleaner that way. There are no lipstick stains, no exchange of body fluids.

I've noticed that women, increasingly, will exchange kisses with new acquaintances, as if it were the feminine version of a handshake. Europeans of both sexes kiss on greeting and parting, but exercise a certain balance by kissing both cheeks.

I put together an informal focus group with some friends—all single—and got everyone talking. Fueled by coffee and cloaked in the promise of anonymity, they shared stories and laughs about the kisses that flavored their lives.

When I requested that our focus be on mouth-to-mouth kissing, someone recalled a study done at Princeton University about five years ago. It proved that our brains are equipped with neurons that help us find our lover's lips in the dark.

Everyone remembers the first kiss, and my kissing pals shared some stories:

"When I was eleven I walked my dog in the park in the evening, and this twelve-year-old boy from the next apartment building came along to protect me. We sat on the bench and he kissed me on the lips. It didn't feel anything like kissing my mother or father or a girl-friend. A month later, the same boy told me about this new French thing, and asked me if I wanted to try it. We did—and broke away from each other squealing. We thought it was gross."

"It was on the porch, after a date. My first kiss was delivered with just the right pressure and timing, but it felt mechanical and was kind of disappointing."

"I remember being afraid to kiss a girl—because I, like most everyone I knew, wore braces. I'd heard horror stories about 'getting stuck.' My buddies told me to just kiss with my lips closed. That worked. After a while I forgot the braces and I tried French kissing, but there were never any lock downs."

"In eighth grade, we had 'make out' parties that were little more than a room full of kids kissing. We played Spin the Bottle and Strawberry Fizz. Someone would make up a story and certain keywords triggered specific kissing actions. When we heard, 'strawberry fizz,' we had license to do *anything*."

Everybody kisses differently and most of us appreciate different kinds of kisses at different times to suit different moods.

Before the group got around to talking about the good stuff, everyone wanted to sound off about what makes for a bad kiss:

"Too much slobber."

"I hate what they call 'the frog,' when the kisser simply sticks the tongue all the way out inside the other's mouth."

"Too many repetitive, wet kisses cause my lips to get chapped."

"I used to date someone who just held his lips against mine, with no motion, just steady pressure. Kissing only one way can be boring."

Hearing this, I informed everyone that there are more than two-hundred fifty references in the *Kama Sutra* to different types of kisses, when to kiss and how to kiss.

Okay, so what kind of kissing *do* people really like?

"It's good when you're kissed in slow, circular motions."

"A good kisser doesn't ask permission but is very sensitive to the reaction. He moves slowly, carefully, paying attention to what she responds to and what seems to turn her off, then adjusts technique accordingly."

"If I open my eyes and find him looking at me, it's so personal. It heightens my awareness of the moment and the person I'm with."

"I like when it starts gentle, but then you start to bite the upper or lower lip and then alternate that with a little tongue action."

When performed well and received with pleasure, kissing signals our brains to produce the hormone oxytocin, an anti-depressive agent that boosts feelings of affection and promotes caretaking behavior.

The best kind of kiss is shared with someone you really care about, but just the act of kissing can stimulate emotions and may bring you closer together. Passionate kisses may be savory, sweet or spicy. Dig in and enjoy.

20

Woman uses her feminine wiles and man is apt to be beguiled

Some women possess an inexplicable power to influence the behavior of men. They use their feminine wiles by revealing strengths and weaknesses in their feminine persona. For many, it's a matter of capitalizing on positive feminine qualities like instinct, communication skill, compassion, empathy and intuition. For others, it involves reverting to helpless-little-girl behavior designed to trigger men's instincts to come to their rescue.

I think it is hardwired into our extra X chromosomes. Our mothers passed on an understanding of how to "work our men." It's been going on since we got men to guard the cave and bring home the bison. When I announced my intention to write about this subject, one woman blurted out, "Oh, don't reveal our secrets!"

Deborah told me about when her four-year-old niece and six-year-old nephew were playing with their Barbie and GI Joe dolls. When Daniel refused to give up the GI Joe, she took her Barbie, sashayed her up to GI Joe and said in a low voice, "Hello soldier."

Deborah said, "We were mystified and amused. My niece is the last little girl you would normally associate with feminine wiles. She is very direct, not at all coy, and she didn't spend afternoons watching World War II movies."

Pouring on the charm usually involves emphasizing our soft, sensual, sexual nature. We become flirtatious. We remind our subjects of our archetypal roles as mother and seductress.

With the rise of feminism, it became politically incorrect to use feminine wiles. Insinuated promises of sexual favors was seen as denigrating to women and was disdained as a mild form of prostitution.

Aralyn, a tall, dark-haired woman with large bones and a no-nonsense attitude, told me, "I have no feminine wiles. I never did. I'd always resent when I'd watch other women, especially blondes, push up their tits and show off how they can bilk a guy of money, or use him for their personal agenda, when they have no other interest in the sucker."

Another friend, Marilyn, echoed her sentiments. "I have no feminine wiles and, if I did, I wouldn't use them."

Other women are proud of their powers. They are a secret resource to be counted on even when the woman lacks physical assets. Tina is struggling with obesity, yet she still boasts about "using the girl card."

"I have never had to change the water bottle at the office even though I use it. I also like to rearrange the furniture in my office periodically and can always get the guys to move it for me. I just mention that I would like to arrange it differently and they offer to help. I stand around and supervise."

A coworker mentioned that she couldn't figure out how Tina always managed to get a seat on the bus, no matter how full it was. "I look at the guys and smile and look so helpless trying to hold on to the pole that one usually gets up and offers his seat to me."

Some women have the knack, others just don't. Carole told me about a college friend who did not want to pump her own gas, even though the woman was bright and capable and certainly knew how. "She'd go over to the pump slowly, stand there looking very confused, catch a guy's eyes and look at him until the guy would come over and pump her gas. It could be any guy, didn't matter, she did it every time.

"I was astounded and asked her how she did it. She said she did it very, very slowly. She had it all figured out, so I tried it to see if I could duplicate her results. I did it as slowly as I could and tried to look extremely confused. After a long wait nobody came over to pump my gas, so I filled up the tank myself. Disgusted, I got back in the car and asked her what I had done wrong. She said I'd been in too much of a hurry. She saw a guy on his way over to help me, but I didn't wait long enough. Sad to say, I never even saw him. That was years ago and no guy has ever come up to me and asked to pump my gas. I'm still waiting."

Do men mind falling prey to feminine wiles? Not the few I asked. Steve put it this way: "I love it when women act coy and flirtatious. It brings out machismo in me. I'm going to help ladies anyway and love when I feel flattered for my efforts."

I can't say that all men enjoy being taken by a woman's tactics. Probably not in the case of this story Pat told about his girlfriend Carolyn. Carolyn was a beautiful girl and had a wild streak. One afternoon she was driving from Austin to Houston to meet Pat at a party. She was already dressed for the party and was running really late. Halfway there, she saw the Department of Public Safety officer's lights in her rearview mirror and cursed her luck. She pulled over and, as she watched the officer get out of his cruiser, she thought to herself, "What the hell." She pulled her miniskirt up a little higher and pulled her top a little lower. When the officer knocked on her window, she rolled down the window, fluttered her eyelashes and cooed, "How can I help you, officer? Are you selling tickets to the policeman's ball?" The officer stopped writing in his ticket book and peered out from behind his reflective sunglasses at her and replied, "No, ma'am, the DPS doesn't have balls."

There was stunned silence for a few moments, and then the DPS officer pushed his glasses back up his nose, smartly snapped his ticket book shut and walked back to his cruiser without another word.

21

Say it the old fashioned way. Express your love in a letter

Want to give your lover a Valentine that will touch their heart? Forget the cards, chocolates and lingerie. Instead, give something that costs only pennies but will be treasured. Write your honey a love letter. No other keepsake could ever be so romantic.

Address it to your girlfriend, boy friend, partner or spouse—or to the new love interest in your life. Love letters can be a great form of flirtation.

At a time when many of our exchanges transpire over the Internet or by cell phone, a love letter makes a most unique and memorable gift. Words written in longhand with ink on paper, bearing your signature, are more tangible and enduring than any spoken.

Does the thought of committing your feelings to paper scare you? We may wrestle with fear that those words will mock us one day or that our offering will not be reciprocated or, worse, will be scorned. If the feelings are there, take the risk. There's no legal liability if your feelings change. The exciting part is experiencing the vulnerability of being so direct.

Don't worry if your writing skills aren't the sharpest. Almost anyone can write a short, personal communiqué. It's not going to be the definitive treatise on your relationship. To the one person who will receive your letter, only the feelings behind the words will matter.

Here are some simple guidelines to help you get started. Try whichever ones appeal to you.

Begin by taking a break from your routine. Go somewhere quiet to write, away from the person to whom you are writing, where you can be alone with your thoughts. If you can't close the door in a room of your own, go to a coffee house. What you're going to put on paper is to be for the eyes of only you and your love.

Take a little time to reflect on your relationship and why you want to please your lover with your message.

The love letter is an expression of your innermost feelings for another person. Use the opportunity to communicate openly, candidly.

Put on paper what's in your heart. Describe how you feel when you are together, or how it is when apart. Address the importance of your relationship in your life. Express why you are grateful for what you share. Say what your friend or spouse means to you and how your life is better and brighter for being together.

Explain why you are writing the letter. Describe what you most admire about your sweetheart. Be clear about what you want the other person to understand about you. And then say what you most want to communicate—whether it is a testament of love, an apology, a desire for greater closeness or simple appreciation.

Remember to make it personal. Insert your beloved's name once or twice. Refer to private moments that only you two know about. Mention the traits you find adorable. Bring up specific qualities or idiosyncrasies you appreciate. Depending on the stage of your relationship, describe your hopes for the future or recall past times together. Praise your lover's performance in bed and proclaim how turned on you get. Describe the soft and tender feelings in your heart when you think of your love. Be affectionate. You are, through your words, making love.

Only say what is true for you, not what you think your lover wants to hear. Find truth in yourself. Select the good feelings, the positive experiences, and document them in your letter.

Avoid the inclination, if you have it, to throw in comments that have an edge. If you feel doubts or have issues about the relationship, save them for when you are face to face in conversation. They don't belong in a love letter.

Write a rough draft on plain note paper. Mull it over and make changes. Use everyday terms and avoid complicated words when simple ones will do.

Spelling accuracy is a must. Misspelled words are symbols of carelessness, which can distract from your message. Read your letter aloud to check for awkward or stilted phrasing.

You can and should free-associate. It's all right to get flowery and to use clichés, even to borrow verse. In this kind of letter, purple prose is desirable.

Should you get locked in writer's block, try speaking into a tape recorder and then transcribing. If you're totally tongue-tied, you can resort to borrowing romantic sentiments. Many web sites, like www.lovingyou.com, provide thousands of sentimental love quotes free for you to crib. But be careful—if you assemble a collection of sweet sentiments drawn only from libraries, your letter will sound canned.

When your note is finished, make a clean copy of it in your most graceful longhand so that the finished letter reflects care and unfaltering conviction. If possible, put the final version on beautiful specialty paper. Selecting colorful or handmade paper shows planning and conveys special value. Even better, create a card yourself, assemble a collage or include your own artwork.

Sprinkle it with your perfume or cologne. Sign it, fold it neatly in an envelope and seal it with a kiss.

Above all, have fun writing to the person of your dreams. Just getting out the words that were bottled up inside you will feel good. Think of the smile it will bring to your sweetheart's face when such a special letter from you is found in the mailbox, carefully tucked into a knapsack or surreptitiously placed under the bed pillow.

"The Letter" (detail) bas-relief,
12" x 14" x 0.5," ceramic, acrylic, wax, 2005

22

Somewhere out there is a man who holds my heart in his hands

I don't know what boys do when thinking about their future mates—but, growing up, an American girl learns to identify and then look for her dream man. Articles in fashion magazines coached us to make a list of the characteristics and qualities our ideal guy would possess and write them down. Deep down inside, we were told, we knew who he was and, once we drew a clear picture, we would certainly recognize him when fate threw us together.

Once we started dating, we couldn't help but notice that the boys in our circle didn't bear much resemblance to our dream man. Some might have had one or two of the qualities that were on our shopping list, but no one delivered them all. Our dream man matured into a distant promise of someone we'd meet when we were fully grown and truly ready for him.

At some point almost every young woman thinks she's met her ideal match. The heady rush of quickened pulse seems proof enough. Something about him is an answer to her prayers. She becomes intent on seduction, blinded by the projection of her fondest desires. Such a romantic jumpstart can lead to a stable relationship—if and when the real man underneath is understood and appreciated. More often, however, disappointment sets in and the hoped-for dream man is forgotten as quickly as are most of our dreams after we awake from sleep.

Eventually, we may exercise emotional intelligence and find rich friendship, romance and love with someone who falls short of our ideal. Gaining instant gratification usually wins over holding out for someone whom we may never meet. Our tastes can change, and we may come to develop an appreciation of low-hanging fruit. If things go well, we may find ourselves with a healthy attraction to someone who doesn't fit our mold exactly, but with whom we can grow, learn and adapt to change. That's what being in a relationship is all about.

Our dream man may go on vacation for years at a time, but he may reappear unexpectedly in our mind's eye. For single and coupled women alike, the dream man is never fully forgotten. He hovers in the recesses of our consciousness, a metric against whom to compare all other males. We don't know a lot about him; the details are fuzzy. But he represents the antithesis of what we don't like in our life.

He may be wealthy, artistic and successful in life. He is considerate of us and others. Or he may be free-spirited and wild, or foreign and mysterious. In our much wished-for association with him, he lifts us out of our humdrum existence with the promise of better times and deeper intimacy. Sometimes he accompanies us in our imaginations, a secret companion.

Ask a grown woman about her dream man and watch closely. Before a word is out of her mouth, you may glimpse on her face a candid look of instant recognition that is quickly erased by a fear of violating a taboo. She's unaccustomed to revealing her secret longings.

For a classic dream man, look no further than actor Rudolph Valentino, the first sex symbol in the history of cinema and a hunk to behold. Valentino's on-screen characters possessed impeccable charm and swashbuckling power, always Johnny-on-the-spot in times of danger. His appreciation for and love of women was legendary and, most important, his sexual appetite went undisguised and women swooned over his exhibition of Latin lust.

Dream man may disappear for a few years, as if on sabbatical. But then he may unexpectedly return to our consciousness. We want to forget him and focus on real men, but he keeps popping up and challenging the choices we've made about who we want to be with. After years of looking for dream man, sometimes it's hard to block him out and make his presence scarce.

We never know much about dream man—just some sketchy highlights such as how he would dance, what his kisses would taste like or how he behaves in a crisis. Since we never see him in real life, he can't do anything to dash our hopes. If we spent more time with him, we would start to become aware of his human foibles—but that won't ever really happen.

The dream man is an archetype that Jungian psychology calls your animus. This person has a magical, eternal quality. When contemplating him, your soul aches with an almost spiritual longing. He appears to you as everything you have ever needed. When you are near him you are lost in rapture; when you are apart, you fall into a pit of darkest despair.

Men, if you've read this far, you probably really want to know what a dream man is supposed to be like. What do you have to do to be the answer to some gal's dream? Listen up:

In a recent on-line survey, the Harris Poll and Dodge Dakota asked 2,131 U.S. adults aged eighteen and over, of whom 1,003 were men and 1,128 were women, to describe the ideal man. Ninety-two percent of women want their man to be dependable—someone on whom they can count. Ninety percent say their ideal man is low-maintenance, easy-going and spends more time fixing things around the house than fixing his own physique. And eighty-eight percent say they want a man who will make them laugh.

23

A sidewalk sex clinic offers
lots of laughter and learning

Ever been to a sex therapist? Neither had I. But when I saw a flier advertising a free sidewalk sex clinic, I couldn't resist going. It was to be held in broad daylight, in front of one of the locations of Forbidden Fruit, a woman-owned local store that sells adult gifts.

On the sidewalk, behind a long table, sat four women waiting to take questions. Two men and two women sat opposite them, wrapped in conversation. And behind them, a cluster of people standing by the parked cars in the street waited to pop their questions.

The crowd was fairly mixed, male and female. It cut across ethnic lines, economic strata and generations. They had come as couples, in same-sex groups and as individuals. A few passersby had spontaneously stopped for a chuckle. And there was a whole lot of giggling going on. Most everyone talking was laughing. The feeling was light-hearted and friendly.

To the right—and you couldn't help looking at her first—was Miss Elise, a local fetish queen. Dressed like a nurse, she donned a nurse's cap, heavy black-framed glasses and a tight white uniform that revealed more cleavage than you can imagine above a white corset that became visible when the buttons on her uniform were unfastened. A sign in front of Ms. Elise stated she could answer questions about BDSM (bondage, dominance, submission and sadomasochism).

Next to her sat Cay Crow, a sex therapist certified by the American Association of Sexuality Educators, Counselors and Therapists (www.aasect.org). Crow teaches a course in human sexuality at San Antonio College and writes a weekly column for the San Antonio Express-News. She had a life-sized, anatomically correct rubber model of female genitals, and a woman was poking her finger inside it—searching for the G-spot, I think.

To the left were Annie Sprinkle and her partner Elizabeth Stephens, performance artists who had conceived and staged free sidewalk sex clinics in New York and San Francisco before bringing them here to Austin. They were answering questions about gay and lesbian sex, as well as hetero, bi and poly.

I yearned to listen in on each set of conversations but, standing around, waiting for a seat to open up, you couldn't make out in the low din what anyone was saying.

What does one talk about with a sex therapist? I imagined: anything! That was the whole idea. You could ask questions, discuss intimate experiences and get expert advice for things so personal you may not even have talked about them with your lover.

When a seat opened up, the folks before me all hesitated. Two men shook their heads. They were waiting to see the nurse. I wound up talking to Crow. It was great. I was as impressed by her ability to put me at ease as I was with her ability to explain the technical aspects of our biochemistry during sexual fantasies. The informed, practical advice I received provoked a flood of additional questions and the sharing of stories and good laughs. It was a relief to have permission to get straight to the point and not beat around the bush when talking about carnal knowledge.

When the two-hour event concluded, I asked the four "sexperts" if they would summarize the questions people had asked and how they answered. Happy to oblige, they said that the sidewalk clinic brought the same kinds of questions they were asked in their regular private practices. Sex therapy is a streamlined form of psychotherapy that focuses exclusively on your sex life.

Elise told me that most people ask her how they can get into a sadomasochism scene: "How can I meet a partner?" "What should I expect?"

"I tell them to join a group in town," Elise says. GWNN.net is the web site for the local Group With No Name and there is also the National Leather Association (NLA) at www.nla-i.org. "I warn them that they won't necessarily have sex or get to play with a partner. These groups have socials in public places, bars or restaurants. You talk, shake hands and listen to announcements. By joining a group you can find out where the parties are." At a party, she tells me, some spanking benches and a St. Andrew's cross (a big X to which you can bind someone) have been set up in a large private room. There's no sex; it's just for playing all kinds of BDSM or Dom and Sub games.

"Like when you're dating, you want to get to know one another first before you go into this intimate process," Elise says. "There are no quick fix-ups. People must learn to trust you and you must learn to communicate openly about what you want or don't want. For example, 'You may call me a slut, but not a whore.'"

Crow said she had received questions about desire discrepancies between couples and about the mechanics of erections and Kegel muscles. "I had to dispel a lot of misinformation people got from the media. I try to get people out of their ruts. Many won't try anything different sexually because they are afraid doing so will disrupt their partner's pleasure. If I suggest a slightly different way, it opens up a lot. There are many routes to pleasure."

Sprinkle and Stephens said they had spoken to a group of four nineteen-year-old guys who came with a female friend. "'Our friend can't have an orgasm,' they said on her behalf. They wanted us to tell them how they could help her," said Sprinkle. "We help people create the kind of sex lives they want to have. But the only answer we can give to everyone is, 'It depends....' Everyone is an entire erotic universe unto themselves."

24

In June, when wedding bells ring, singles are pressed to marry too

At a recent dinner party, I found myself seated at a table with multiple generations. The grown children of my friends were talking about the pressures they were feeling to settle down and get married. In June, each had been invited to so many weddings that the topic could not be avoided. Too many well-wishers were asking, "So when is your turn?"

Julia and Jason were in separate, long-term, committed relationships. Both were attractive, well educated and enjoyed promising careers. Julia was impatient to get engaged to Brian and frustrated that a proposal hadn't been made yet. Jason was getting ready to pop the question to his girlfriend, but he found himself under so much pressure from her and others that it made him want to drag his heels.

I saw Julia and Jason as being on opposite sides of the same coin. Both were acting out roles typical of their genders. Both agreed to be interviewed separately about their respective attitudes toward getting married.

Julia said that she and Brian had been together for six years; she was twenty-seven and he was a year older. She recalled how they met when he was still with his high school sweetheart of six years. Together they had grown up, fallen in love and lost their virginity. They were at the point where the girl wanted to get married; he wasn't sure he was quite ready for that, and then Julia appeared on the scene. Julia admits that she facilitated their breakup.

Now Julia and Brian have been living together a little more than a year. "We're currently saving for and planning to buy a house. I don't want to do that until we're engaged," she said.

Julia recalled that their first two years were heated and tumultuous. There were many fights, a lot of passion and a roller coaster of ups and downs. He's a very gentle, introverted, calm person whose family rarely expressed emotion or affection. She is fiery, having come from an emotionally effusive family. Brian didn't want to be around a lot of drama; he shrank from people who yelled.

"He's still holding old stuff against me even though I've grown and changed a lot," says Julia. "Brian recognizes that this is a good union for him, but he may have lingering fears that, ten years down the road, when it does get harder and the passion fades a little, we'll have a tumultuous relationship again. I can't get him to admit it, but I'm pretty sure that's what's going on." His hesitancy causes her to worry about how much longer she'll be able to have kids.

"I am not going to wait forever," she said. "I won't do this for another two years. But I don't think I have really said that to him."

Julia said that Brian believes she wants to get married for what he considers to be the wrong reasons: for security, to gain approval from friends and family, and because their friends are getting married and she's feeling left out.

"I try hard not to make the issue of marriage our dinner conversation, but it is something that we talk about more frequently than ever. My best friend just got married, and a childhood friend got engaged—in situations like that, the issue definitely comes up. It's becoming a hot button for me, but it's not for Brian."

I wasn't too surprised that Jason was harder to pin down for an interview than Julia, and that he had less to say. Unlike Julia, who said she could talk about it all day, Jason never discusses the M-word with friends.

Jason and his girlfriend moved in together a year ago with the understanding that it was a precursor to marriage. But, he says, "We really moved in for convenience. We met in medical school and knew we'd be in this location doing residencies for at least six years. We wanted to buy a house.

"The subject of marriage has become a relatively frequent topic of conversation," says Jason. "She's basically waiting for me to propose. When the subject comes up, I'm not surprised. I just feel that she's in more of a hurry than I am. When we attend weddings, it ratchets up the tension.

"I want more time. This year has been a big change for us. We're living more professional lives and have less free time. I don't have a lot of savings, and weddings are expensive. Rings and honeymoons cost money. But the main reason I haven't proposed yet is that I want to first make sure I'm ready emotionally to make that kind of commitment. We know each other pretty well. I'm not expecting anything to change. I just need to convince myself that we'll be successful together in marriage and in life."

His hesitation, he says, stems from wanting to be certain this is the right relationship for him and from what may be a lack of enthusiasm for the institution of marriage in general. "I don't want to have to deal with being divorced," he says. "And if you study the animal kingdom, you'll see that males are not biologically wired for being with one person. It's not in our nature."

In contrast, Julia admits, "It's funny. If you eliminate the whole issue of marriage, I'm almost completely happy and content in this relationship. Brian's my best friend, my lover, my partner. He satisfies my needs. We get along great. I love his family. He loves mine. But there's this huge thing that is missing and, at this point, that is overshadowing the whole relationship."

"After the Ball" (detail) bas-relief,
11.5" x 9.5" x 1," ceramic, 2005

$\mathcal{P}$art III

25

Look out for Number One and relationships suffer

The crossroads where the political and the personal meet is a place where I turn my attention. That's what drew me to hear what Rabbi Michael Lerner had to say. He's the editor of *Tikkun,* a Jewish magazine; author of *The Left Hand of God: Taking Back Our Country From the Religious Right;* and is involved in organizing a political movement called The Network of Spiritual Progressives.

I went to a lecture he gave, bought his book, caught him on *Meet the Press,* and joined the network's e-mail list. I had a strong inner sense of recognizing truth when I heard what he had to say—not just about politics, but about personal, romantic relationships.

Lerner challenges the political left to give up its deeply held fear of religion and to distinguish between a domination-oriented, Right-Hand-of-God tradition, and a more compassionate and hope-oriented Left-Hand-of-God world view. He says that the Democratic Party must rethink its relationship to God, champion a progressive spiritual vision, reject the old bottom line that promotes the globalization of selfishness, and deal head-on with the very real spiritual crisis that affects our entire Western society.

"I had interviewed ten thousand middle-income working families and learned in detail about the way in which, spending day after day in a world of work, the bottom line is to maximize money and power, " says Lerner. "People learn that the common sense of our economy is to look out for Number One. Nobody else is there to protect you. You see other people from the standpoint of what they can do for you, how they can be of use. This utilitarian, instrumental way of looking at the world comes home to our personal lives, where it undermines personal relationships and families."

One of the symptoms of this spiritual crisis is that people feel that their friendships and relationships are becoming thinner and more selfish. There is increased competition for our attention. We are taught to network instead of to form real friendships. We're coached only to give what we can expect to get back. We accept that this is the way the world works, but it leaves us cynical about the quality of friendships and we feel increasingly isolated. Lerner's research shows that people yearn to be valued and loved for themselves and their deeper qualities.

In his book, Lerner reflects on the decades of the nineteen-sixties and -seventies, during which he, I and millions of other baby boomers pursued sex without repression, and concludes, "What we were desperately seeking was not sex but love and the experience of being recognized at our soul's deepest level, and that required a deeper commitment to the other than the sexual freedom the period had encouraged."

Romantic relationships exist in what Lerner refers to as the "dating supermarket," the aisles filled with endless options available for meeting and sampling new partners to see what experiences they might offer. Marriage commitments are based, he says, on a judgment call about who, out of the pool of all possible partners, will meet the most needs.

Not only does such a utilitarian, manipulative approach diminish the sweetness of becoming sweethearts but it sets a couple up for failure. Both partners feel insecure and fear that they could be beat out by future competition that's younger, richer or more attractive.

This led me to examine my own inner motivations and to see what was really there. Had my husband and I picked each other to further our own goals? Was I still counting on him in this respect? To whatever extent I did, I concluded that it would sabotage our relationship, and who needs that? Feelings of blame and resentment dissolved as I recalled the commitment we had made to each other, and I started seeing beyond myself. I believe that consciousness begins locally with those we love and, as we get better at supporting our commitment to the well-being of another, we can extend concern from our most intimate partner to all the people around the world.

Lerner does offer a brighter, more hopeful view for relationships. In an interview with Andrew Cohen for the online magazine *What is Enlightenment?* (www.wie.org), he said, "The fundamental reality of the universe is that we are all interconnected as part of the unity of all Being. And the alienation that we experience is first and foremost an alienation from who we are. It is a product of our failure to understand ourselves as connected to all other human beings and then to all other beings."

Lerner laments how our society today validates that which can be measured through sense data. Everything else is seen as irrelevant or literally "non-sense." That plays into an ethos of selfishness. What can be counted is money, but what cannot be measured is love, kindness and generosity.

Lerner and his Network of Spiritual Progressives are calling for a new bottom line in society. He says, "All religious and spiritual traditions of the human race have a common wisdom that can be applied as a counter to the selfishness and materialism that dominates the old bottom line. We need a new bottom line of love and caring and kindness and generosity. Our capacity to connect with other human beings—every single interaction that we have—is shaped by our consciousness of the totality of human relationships."

Virginity isn't all it once was. What does it mean to us now?

It was expected, when I was a girl, that I would be a virgin on my wedding night. When I reached puberty, however, the sexual revolution was in full swing. I was a little slow in signing on. By the time I was ready to give up my "flower," as it was euphemistically referred to, none of the guys I knew were interested in being with a virgin. As soon as one would realize what a big emotional load was riding on it for me, he'd drop me and run. This caused a dilemma and delayed my first experience a couple of years until I met someone with whom I would have perfect memories. But that is another story.

Doing it for the first time is always a big deal, though I think it now happens earlier.

Rachel, now twenty-eight, recalls, "I realized it was the one thing in my life I could really control. Young, living under my parents' roof, decisions were made for me. Losing my virginity was one decision *I could make*. It was empowering to know I would have sex. But I didn't have access to contraception and the gravity of getting pregnant struck me, so I waited until I was eighteen to become sexually active."

Laurie, twenty-three, says, "I grew up in the post-feminist age, when our bodies were very visible. My friends and I felt it was okay to derive pleasure, but I wanted to be in control. I didn't want rumors circulating about me in school. As a high school freshman, I had sex for the first time just to get it over with. After a couple of experiences that weren't so great, I didn't do it again until I had a long-term relationship in college. I thought, 'Why can't we just make out?' I had access to condoms in high school, and friends would come to me for them."

Parents today tell me they *wish and hope* their children would wait until they were seventeen, but they know that often it doesn't work out that way. Today, most kids have their first sexual experience by the time they are fifteen or sixteen, I'm told by a father of a girl who's sixteen going on twenty-six.

The FDA has approved a new vaccine to protect against transmission of genital warts and recommends that it is most effective when administered before sexual activity begins, at *age nine*. Not only are kids having sex earlier, they're having it more often and talk openly with each other about sex.

They even have "blow job parties." These are a new national phenomenon, Catherine, twenty-nine, informs me. "Kids do it in their bedrooms, basements, closets. Girls get color coded bracelets that show what they would do. Parents don't know the code."

Catherine says it's very hard to be in college as a virgin. She had two virgin friends for whom it's been hard to keep boy friends. One lost it at age twenty-three, the other is still a virgin at twenty-five.

She also knows two male virgins in their thirties and says, "They have very underdeveloped social skills.

"Most kids lose their virginity by the time they're done with high school—despite the policy, here in Texas, of abstinence-only education. Sex education is delivered during just two weeks in a single-semester required health class. I wish that kids were learning how to be responsible and protect their bodies. With abstinence-only education, they don't learn anything about contraception or protection from sexually transmitted diseases."

"Wouldn't it be great," says Laurie, "if the schools taught positive self-image and communication and offered classes in how to be sexual and enjoy it?"

The pendulum is swinging the other way. In response to contemporary promiscuity in the era of AIDS, movements such as True Love Waits, which asks teenagers to refrain from sex before marriage, are heavily subscribed. But the *Journal of Adolescent Health* reports that surveys of sexual behavior after the program indicate an increase in the practice of oral and anal sex and promise breakers are less likely than others to use contraception during their first sexual intercourse experience.

By the most standard modern-day definition, when people talk about a "virgin," they're talking about someone who has not had sexual intercourse of the penis-and-vagina variety. Rachel says that the definition blurs, because kids today may do everything but that. "Gay and lesbian kids are sexually active. Technically, they may be virgins—but I wouldn't call them that."

Virginity (or abstinence) pledges are commitments made by teenagers and young adults to refrain from sexual intercourse until marriage. They are most common in the United States, especially among Evangelical Christian denominations. Often they involve ceremonies in which teenagers wear rings given to them by their parents. Organizations like the Sexuality Information and Education Council of the United States have called abstinence-only programs "fear-based" and "designed to control young people's sexual behavior by instilling fear, shame, and guilt."

Judith Levin, a civil libertarian who helped found the National Writers League, says abstinence educators escalate their messages: "Like advertising, which must continually jack up its seduction just to stay visible as other advertising proliferates, abstinence education had to make sex scarier and scarier and, at the same time, chastity sweeter."

27

After twenty years of marriage new life and new loves lie ahead

The tracks my friend Patti and I have traveled lead in opposite directions socially. I had lived alone for years and dated many men before settling into marriage at age forty. Patti, on the other hand, had never been on her own until age forty. Five years ago her marriage ended after nearly two decades.

"My ex and I still love each other," she told me, "but we both realized that the relationship was no longer feeding our souls. Our two boys were grown and it was time to move on."

She did not view the divorce as a sign of failure, but rather as an exciting opportunity to discover herself. She sounds practically euphoric about her new life.

She admits that she likes being able to make choices for herself without worrying about others. "For the first time, I was not caught in the triangle of husband, kids and job," she says. "Instead of always focusing my energy on one of them, I now really am happy to explore being in my own space."

That space is now filled with music, poetry, art and romantic possibilities. She quit her corporate job and used her savings and her share of the divorce settlement to build a small house out by the lake. Alone, with her dog, she feels safe in the solitude.

"The first thing I do each day is write a haiku. In the morning, I hear only the songs of birds while I write verse. In the evening, I swim. I practice my mandolin and piano. I joined a choir and love to sing when alone at home. I have lots of friends with whom I dance."

She enrolled in school to become a massage therapist. In addition to doing bodywork, she supports herself with a variety of jobs: bookkeeping, waiting tables and tending gardens for some neighbors.

"In massage school we created really deep personal relationships but, for a couple of years, I had no interest in getting involved with anyone. I wanted to discover who I was on my own. But now, almost every man I meet is a romantic possibility.

"Normally, I'm not that focused on being with a man. If someone is there, great. If not, that's fine too."

Patti built a network of women friends. They'd meet regularly for potluck dinner and what they called "resource banking." Each woman talked about what she needed help with.

"I need a job."

"I need support to stop drinking."

"I need a truck."

"I need someone to call after I've been away on business."

Somehow, each woman found what she needed from others in the group.

"With that kind of support," says Patti, "I could be with men and not feel dependent on them for anything. It was very liberating. I had taken my life into my own hands." To date, she's been sexually active with three men. Eugene was the first.

"We met on a Sunday morning at Body Choir, where I love to dance barefoot, wordless but communicating. After the dance, a group of us went out to the lake to canoe. A sudden storm came up and Eugene and I sought shelter on the shore, huddling together under the canoe. Then we went to my place to dry off and warm up. Eugene was sixty, much older than I am—but he had a gorgeous body. I loved his touch, his deep woody smell. I have never had such great sex with anyone before or after. He was very spiritual in an unconventional way. He touched my soul deeply. I felt him stirring things inside me. He got into my pores."

After six months, the intensity was too much for Patti. She tries to be open, but admits she is cautious.

"I couldn't be so cemented down with someone who needed a deep connection on a daily basis. He got *too* close. He wanted to know things that I felt weren't his business. It was all very new, and I needed to leave him to remain independent and have my alone time. We are still friends, but now he's living with another lady and I'm happy for him."

The sexual intensity she experienced with Eugene was not repeated with either of the men with whom she's recently been intimate. "I could relax with them; being with them was and is comforting," she says. "How lovely just to cuddle—and how disappointing."

I told Patti I was relieved to have married soon after AIDS became a known threat and changed my casual behavior. Was she worried, I asked, about the risk of getting a sexually transmitted disease?

"It scares me to death!" she says. "I'm as frightened of getting herpes as I am of getting AIDS, even though I know that they are not equally life threatening."

After marrying young, she knew that she had no communicable diseases. Still, after the first time she slept with her current lover, he phoned to tell her that he had developed a painful sore on his bottom.

"Hearing that really flipped me out," she says. "I was so angry with myself for having gotten involved and with him for putting me in jeopardy." The threat proved to be a false alarm. They both had blood tests taken and the results came back negative for herpes. "It caused me to do a lot of soul searching. I don't want to be diseased or to find out too late about having been exposed. Since I'm not going to live like a hermit, there's so much to educate myself about.

"You meet someone and feel strong emotions about him. You feel lust and want to share your body. When you do there is a risk, but life is full of risks." Patti told me that she has learned much about herself and feels there is still much to learn. She is arranging to rent out her house next year in order to travel indefinitely.

"I'm done with nesting," she says and stretches out her arms like the wings of a great bird. "I'm ready to take flight."

"Strive" (detail) 3" x 3.75" x 11," bronze, 2002

28

Courtship rituals and dating: Just hanging out or mating?

When Dahlia reentered the dating world after thirteen years of marriage, it wasn't what she remembered. "Now the men I meet don't want to go on dates," she says. "Some want to spend time with me, but they say they just want to hang out. I don't know what that means, 'hang out.' One man I've been seeing just likes to come over to my place but we don't have any plans or agenda. I feel like I'm running a bed and breakfast for him."

Dahlia's friend, Margie, echoes her frustration. "It's not like I want a guy to lavish me with fancy restaurants. If we go out, we can go Dutch, but I want him to do something to express his interest in me," says Margie. "I want an indication that he looks forward to seeing me and considers the time we spend together to be special. It's important to me that he shows some creativity or that he put some thought into what I might like."

In the nineteenth century, formal courtship involved a young man calling at a young woman's home and meeting her family. In the twentieth century, consumerism took over and dating took youngsters outside the safe confines of home into movie theaters, restaurants, clubs and bars. Today courtship no longer occupies a vital place in contemporary American culture; the word itself now seems quaint and outdated.

Sure, we possess a certain sense of what the gender roles should encompass, but these lines are becoming increasingly blurred. Several friends, both male and female, have mentioned that the dynamics of courtship have changed significantly since the time when a guy had to call before Wednesday to land a date for Saturday night dinner.

A male student at the University of Texas observed, "People either just start hanging out together and hooking up or they live together, and they are boy friend and girlfriend. Nothing's formal, everything's casual. Dates don't really exist anymore. No one says, 'I'll pick you up at seven.'"

"Some couples hardly ever go anywhere together," says Carol Weston, author of *Private and Personal* and *Girltalk*. "Rather than go out just the two of them, they meet at parties or clubs or coffee shops or sports events or someone's home or apartment. Casual is okay, but take the pulse of your relationship and make sure it has a little romance to it. It's great that girls and guys both have equal rights and both have spending money, but a formal date can be great, too," she says. "If you're always, always, always, going out with friends, you may be missing out on the fun of going out just the two of you."

What's so bad about the dating ritual? On the condition of anonymity, one guy told me, "I don't want to be obliged to spend fifty-plus dollars for a nice dinner or for drinks and a show, or forty if we go for cheap ethnic food and a movie, just to be able to have two hours of conversation with someone and maybe not even get laid. Why do we need to be entertained all the time? That's not real life. In real life you stay home, you visit friends, you cook a meal together. I hope to find someone with whom I can spend the rest of my life, so I want to test run what that would be like. I shouldn't have to buy a woman's company."

Karen Thompson, a psychologist and relationships coach, says dating can be a way to express your creativity and get to know each other rather quickly at what she calls "the essence level." Rather than do the standard dinner and a movie, Thompson invites singles to go more deeply into who they really are and design a date in keeping with their inner spirits. For example, Thompson recently spent time with a new love interest at a movement class. There, she and her date danced in creative, experimental ways—individually, as a couple, and in groups. It was energizing, fun and in keeping with her inner spirit's appreciation of movement and high-energy activity.

In another example, one woman recounted how she and her boy friend planned a day trip to the town where she had grown up. Going there opened the way for lots of tales about what her life was like. They drove past the house where she grew up, stopped at her high school and went for a swim in the creek where she used to play.

Since he didn't grow up locally, she caught a glimpse of his world in another way. He was rugged and liked to hike and camp, so they planned another date—to climb Enchanted Rock. His behavior along the trail—offering to carry her extra water bottles, identifying fauna and flora that he had studied, politely helping her up steep climbs—demonstrated that he was concerned about her comfort and enjoyment and that she could feel secure in his company.

Another couple had an intimate encounter when they went to a local sculpture academy for an evening workshop in which they made plaster face casts of one another. Taking turns, they coated each other's cheeks, mouths, eyes and noses with thick, quick-drying plaster. They allowed their date to stick straws up their nostrils so they could breathe until they gently peeled off the masks. Afterward, they talked about how it felt giving and receiving. They found this to be a very intimate experience, shared in a perfectly safe, fun environment. They each went home with their own mask, each hoping that the relationship would evolve until the two masks wind up mounted side by side in their shared home.

29

Does unequal division of labor create division between lovers?

The latest data from the U.S. Bureau of Labor Statistics ccon-firms what I have always suspected: Women do more housework than men. On an average day in 2005, eighty-four percent of women and sixty-five percent of men spent some time doing household activities such as housework, cooking, lawn care or financial and other household management. On an average day, nineteen per-cent of men reported doing housework—such as cleaning or doing laundry—compared with fifty-three percent of women. Thirty-seven percent of men did food preparation or cleanup versus sixty-six percent of women.

Men also goof off more. Nearly everyone (ninety-six percent) age fifteen and over reported doing some sort of leisure or sports activity, such as watching TV, socializing or exercising. Among this group of participants, men spent more time doing leisure activities (five-point-seven hours) than women (five hours).

It doesn't seem balanced or fair, does it?

Housework is one of the most common causes of arguments. It may seem a trivial thing to fall out about, but some couples are willing to pay for counseling to sort it out.

Others can afford to hire someone else to do the dirty work. Still, even with weekly housekeeper visits, there's still underwear to be picked up, sinks to be cleaned, garbage to be dumped and dishes done.

Bickering about housework sometimes masks a deeper fear that you are not loved or respected. Love and respect are essential ingredients in a relationship. Sometimes housework becomes the battleground where you fight for these needs to be fulfilled.

With or without professional counseling, it's a good idea to look at what causes you upset. Discuss it to learn more about yourself and your partner. Is one of you expecting "mom" to always be there to pick up after you? Talk without accusation, using "I" statements and describing your own experience. Describe how a situation makes you feel and how you would *like* to feel. It may help you work things out, and you may wind up with a clean house as a bonus!

We're taught that part of loving someone is looking after their physical needs. It's personal, a way of demonstrating that you care.

When I was growing up, women did all the housework, including cooking, cleaning and laundry. Men did repairs and looked after the yard. Period.

Thankfully, things have changed; roles aren't as sexually stereo-typed. Now couples often share the household duties. They each do the chores they prefer or those at which they excel. Ideally, they agree to take turns doing the chores no one wants to do.

It's not always so simple. Sometimes one party winds up taking out the cat litter repeatedly without the other lifting a finger to help, even when it's obvious that the bin is full and stinks. So the party that gets stuck with the cat poop feels disadvantaged and compromised.

An all-too-common response is to nag, to compile lists of "honey dos," to constantly remind the cohabitant of what needs to be done. How can he be so forgetful? How can she be such a shrew?

It's usually easier to let it go and just do the chore. It's an opportunity to examine why you chose your partner. What else is good that makes you stay together despite such ongoing irritations? Most people find plenty to appreciate when they make the effort to reflect. Doing so can help you to affirm your love.

Everyone loves appreciation, especially when it is mutual. Showing yours is the best way to enroll someone in helping out. Doing a task yourself to spare the one you love is a great way to demonstrate appreciation. What's important is that you feel appreciated and are able to appreciate.

Housework can be uplifting. Not only does it create a clean, calm, inviting space in which to share your life together, it can be a process for centering and raising awareness.

It's all in the way you approach it. Try doing your housework with no expectations, no agenda and no thinking. Do it as a service for the benefit of the greater community and you can clean your *karma* while you clean the floors. While sorting laundry, sort out your own inner confusion. Treat it as a meditation, and by doing so experience the joy of being in the present moment. You may find that your senses are more alive and you feel more energetic and good about yourself when you're done.

Find your own rhythms for doing housework. I know a husband and wife who both work from home. She'll do chores whenever she needs a break from her computer. That multitasking would distract him, so he does concentrated housework on Saturdays.

Some couples enjoy doing housework together. Some do it nude and make it a game of "Maid and Master" or "Mistress and House Boy."

In preparation for writing his book, *VoiceMale: What Husbands Really Think About Their Marriages, Their Wives, Sex, Housework, and Commitment,* Neil Chethik surveyed three hundred American husbands and conducted in-depth interviews with seventy men in all stages of marriage. In a *Newsweek* interview, he states that there's a "parallel between housework and sex…Men said the happier their wives were in the division of housework, the happier the men were with their sex lives."

I'll speculate that this division of labor extends to the bedroom. A partner who is lazy about the chores is also apt to be lazy in bed. And you wouldn't want to be with someone who lets you do all the work.

30

One-on-one relationships versus consensual non-monogamous love

Is it possible to have a loving, committed romantic relationship that involves more than two people? It goes contrary to some of our deepest cultural convictions about the virtues of marriage and monogamy. Yet many people have relationships with multiple partners, and some say that this kind of love works for them.

It's called polyamory, and it has moved from being a utopian dream to being a real, though fringe, social practice. The Internet has allowed previously isolated individuals and groups interested in or practicing various forms of polyamory to meet others, to communicate about lifestyle issues and to organize local and national groups of like-minded people. Poly-Austin claims that nearly six hundred members are in its Yahoo! group. A magazine devoted to polyamory, Loving More (www.lovemore.com), has a national audience. On and off the web, a polyamorous community is developing.

Advocates insist that polyamory is different from cheating, which involves deceit. Polyamory is characterized by free and responsible choice, with the mutual informed consent of all involved.

It is distinct from polygamy, being rooted in such concepts as trust, equality and freewill, rather than cultural or religious traditions.

No one person can fill all your needs is an argument that's hard to beat.

Polyamorous relationships are as varied as the individuals in them. Some are *vees, triangles, quads* or *moresomes*. They may all pile into one bed, or they may never meet the others in the equation. Relationships can be further complicated when the attraction is to someone whose gender is not the same as that of the current partner. A tacit "Don't ask, don't tell" policy works for some. Others agree to introduce and ask for approval from the first love for the new love. The most common form of polyamory is the primary-secondary model, in which one relationship is considered primary and takes precedence over other relationships that may form. The rules of the game usually evolve out of discussion, empathy and practice—which makes it a lot like good lovemaking.

Polys (as they call themselves) hold that love is infinite. The more love given, the more there is to share. Monogamy, they complain, is based on the premise that love comes in limited supply. If you give your love to one person, there is none left to give to anyone else. Then if you fall in love with another, you pay by withdrawing your love from the first party.

Love may be limitless in the abstract, but there *is* a finite number of people that one can love and spend time with; the emotional resources available to anybody are not without bounds. Everyone's schedule must be accommodated. It's best to venture into polyamory when your relationships and relationship skills are already strong.

Non-monogamy is such a threat to conventional relationships that people are forced into being closeted about their affairs. There are strains that accompany the keeping of so large and important a secret. There is the fear of being discovered and shunned by people who might disapprove. There is the stress that comes from insufficient recognition of one's partners. For example, the partner who is not invited to family gatherings and office parties may feel excluded and devalued. Increasingly, some polys *come out*, just as do homosexuals.

Multiple partner relationships are not without jealousy. Most polys, however, regard the emotion as a signal that something needs investigation and care, much as they would regard depression or pain. A poly relationship depends on mutual security and trust. Ideally, it involves *compersion*—a term used by practitioners of polyamory for taking pleasure when one's partner is with another person.

Challenging as it may be to engage in group relations, there are many benefits. More of a person's interests can be met, and those interests may even expand when there are multiple people with whom to do things. There is an extended support network. Increased self-awareness may come when multiple partners call you on your bullshit. In polyamory there's less room for personal insecurities and co-dependent communication patterns. At the same time, it's easier to maintain individual identity when you aren't always in lock-step with one other person.

While openly polyamorous relationships are relatively rare, de-mographic studies indicate that private polyamorous arrangements within relationships are actually quite common. In one study of over thirty-five hundred married couples, as many as twenty-eight per-cent had an understanding that allows non-monogamy under some circumstances. The percentages were higher among cohabitating lesbian and gay couples.

Polyamory adds a layer of complexity to the already complex job of managing a romantic relationship. Those involved in such relationships tend to gain a lot of practice communicating their needs and negotiating arrangements that are satisfactory to all. There's a sense of pride among those who can meet the challenges that come with loving more than one. Support groups offer help in transcending jealousy, communicating authentically, meeting lovers, raising kids in polyamorous households, learning about rights—including marriage—for those in non-monogamous unions. For more about polyamory visit www.polyamorysociety.org.

"Seated Female Nude (Melissa)" (detail)
12" x 9.5" x 15," ceramic, acrylic, wax, 2004

31

Talking about sex with your lover adds to the pleasure

Most of us understand that open communication is the key to good relationships. So why then do we find ourselves at a loss for words when it comes to sex?

A woman seems to expect her partner to gaze longingly into her eyes and glean exactly how she wants him to get her off. A man often won't say anything about sex for fear of offending the "delicate nature" of his partner or of being called a "degenerate."

Talking about sex may be a turn-on for some, but it takes some of us out of our comfort zone. For shy people, explicitly sexual talk is like a foreign language—but it's one that can be learned and enjoyed. If you can describe what turns you on, you're much more likely to have your desires met.

For insight and advice on the topic I turned to Cay Crow, a certified sex therapist who has a private counseling practice in Central Texas and teaches human sexuality at San Antonio College.

Our inhibition about talking about sex stems from our puritanical heritage, she says. "Someone who talked openly about sex was thought to be immoral. It's a contradiction that, when in a relationship, we feel free to act sexually but not to talk about it. Talking involves acknowledging and owning your desires."

To initiate a discussion about any problems you may have or to give feedback about what you like, Crow recommends going to a neutral setting outside the bedroom, when you are both free from interruptions. "Some women have issues with what they can tolerate in terms of vaginal lubrication and vigorous sexual behavior. Some men may have problems with erectile dysfunction or premature ejaculation. If you have a medical issue that interferes with your sexual functioning and you just keep going on as if nothing was wrong, you could really end up seriously harming yourself. You need to talk, to tell your partner if there is a problem, if you need more lubrication or if you need to go slower."

Be specific. Let your partner know exactly what you would like to do, such as make love outside, or have your partner watch you while you stimulate yourself. Ask what your partner would enjoy. Ask whether hearing you talk about sex is exciting.

If you encounter resistance, Crow suggests that you both try the following exercise: "Compile a list of words that turn you on and another list of words that turn you off. Sharing the list with your partner can help in beginning a conversation about sex. Ask your partner why certain words are appealing and others are not; you may learn something about your partner that you weren't aware of."

Words have the power to arouse. There are two kinds of oral sex. If you know what you're doing, both achieve the same result.

Try adding a sound track to the action in the bedroom. Moan appreciatively when something feels good. Gasp, growl, breathe loudly, whimper, let out a scream. Making noise heightens your partner's pleasure as well as your own and provides useful and encouraging feedback. A couple of well-timed "Oh yes, oh yes!" sighs can take you far.

Raunchy talk during sex helps us to keep a connection between body and mind. A good play-by-play announcer can heighten the general excitement of the match, provided a few rules are observed. Simply announce, in an urgent but straightforward way, exactly what you're doing, along with a scattering of hints about what to look for next.

Remember that there is a wide range of salacious words, from the mild to the hard-core. Individual preferences vary. Figure out where on the scale your partner's preference falls and stay within that range.

Start by describing what is going on between your legs and move on to what is going on between your ears. It can make you feel sexy to say certain things in bed that you imagine saying in your fantasies. Just because you describe a fantasy doesn't mean that you have to act it out. Acting it out can destroy a fantasy, but preserved jointly by two imaginations, a fantasy can be doubly exciting.

"Fantasies come from a part of the psyche that is extremely wild," says Crow. "You don't always know what will come out, but it doesn't mean you're a bad person because you desire something."

Being embarrassed by something and being turned off or upset by it are two different things. If you or your partner are shy, Crow suggests a way to initiate a conversation about sex that is especially useful: "Each of you composes a list with three columns. In the first column, list the sexual activities in which you would like to engage. In the second column, list sexual activities you would consider trying. And in the third column, list sexual activities that are outside your level of comfort. Sharing the lists will give you an idea of the sexual boundaries of the relationship. You may be surprised by your partner's list, but you must respect those desires even if they do not match your own. From the list of things that you both would try, choose a new activity every week, or every month."

Should you run out of things to say, erotic fiction and the Internet can provide an endless supply of inspiration. Finding out what others are doing and thinking will encourage you to expand your sexual vocabulary.

Whether you are whispering in her ear or barking orders at him, words have special power. They open the way into more than just the other person's body; they let you into your lover's mind. Listen up and listen well.

32

Bring on the dancing girls!
'Dirty dancing' gains respect

Once the bailiwick of strip joints, gentlemen's clubs and bachelor parties, exotic dancing is now being performed in homes, apartments and condos across our land. Tens of thousands of women have joined in classes—for women only—that teaches how to make the moves and do the old bump and grind. *The New York Times* reports that over the past ten years, "Pole dancing, once exclusively the province of exotic dancers, has flared up as a much-hyped Hollywood exercise craze, and has seeped into the collective unconscious through shows like *The Sopranos* and *Desperate Housewives*."

I took the class from Donna Starnes, who teaches The Art of Exotic Dancing for Everyday Women at her fitness studio, NiaSpace in South Austin. There are now more than fifty instructors teaching exotic dancing in twenty states. Some twenty of us showed up for class on a sunny Saturday afternoon, all a little excited about being there—and a little nervous. The class began with women doing what we do best: sitting in a circle and sharing why we were there and how we felt about it. We were a mixed group: college students and menopausal matrons and everything in between, all shapes, sizes and colors in varying levels of fitness. One gal was five months pregnant. Some of us came on our own, wanting to learn to do exotic dance for our husbands, others wanting to find a way to stand out on a crowded dance floor.

Donna then shared her dance and was so clearly having fun, it was inspiring. Then she turned on a mix of dance music (so we could find hear what we liked most) and we started learning the moves. We did the alluring and hip accentuating step-drag-walk, four kinds of hip rolls and "floorplay"—moving through a series of provocative poses—and we learned how to put it all together into a dance. We wore high heels, played with colorful feather boas and practiced wriggling out of a big shirt. There was no right or wrong way to perform. Each woman could make up her own dance, a personal expression of her individual sexual dynamism. We lit up. In the large mirrors on each wall, we could watch ourselves transform from Plain Janes into Sexy Salomes.

"Women come to the class expecting just to learn some moves they can perform for their partners," says Starnes, "but in addition to that, they start feeling empowered, strong and confident. We teach eye-contact exercises, which helps each one get a sense of her own inner beauty." Practicing with mirrors as we made eye contact with ourselves while gyrating, we became the arbiters of our own beauty rather than looking to someone else for positive reinforcement.

Starnes tells a story about one student in the class who was extremely overweight, three hundred pounds. She hadn't had a date in years, not even an advance. She took the class and, on the way home on the public bus, some guy came along, struck up a conversation and asked her out. She had shifted her energy so that her inner beauty was showing and the attraction occurred.

On the web site for the class, www.artofexoticdancing.com, it says, "The Art of Exotic Dancing lessons are a gateway to your most feminine self, your true essence." As I watched myself and my classmates in the mirrors, I saw our beauty, sensuality, wildness and confidence increase. Rather than acting as if we were sexually subjugated as we imagined dancing for a man, we demonstrated a natural power to tempt, delight and control our audience. It was easy and fun. The eye-contact exercise was particularly potent. When we dance suggestively and get really personal by making eye contact, we say so much about our availability, interest and erotic potential. I was particularly taken with one of my classmates, a proper and tightly laced thirty-something graduate student from India, who turned into a playful, voluptuous siren when she practiced a dance she intended to show her husband that night.

Doing a dance performance in the privacy of your own home is vastly different from being a pole dancer in a club on the side of a freeway. Not that I've been to one of those seedy places myself, but the prude in me feels disdain for the patrons whom, I hear, tuck ten dollar bills into the g-strings of the dancers as rewards for gratifying behavior. That's so degrading and impersonal.

Most men are so easily aroused by visual stimuli. When a man sees a woman dance it will fuel his lust and help him to release some tension. Yet one man confided in me that he was intimidated and embarrassed by these dancers. Men in his office would use his birthday as an excuse to drag him, the only bachelor, to a strip club. The impersonal nature of it was a turnoff to him.

It is, however, deeply personal and a definite turnon when you're dancing for your lover and showing a side of yourself no one else can see. What's different is that, when your dance is over, you don't get dressed and go home alone, as all twenty of us did when the class was over. Your improvisation continues, you invite your lover to join you and, together, you dirty dance your way into the bedroom.

33

A lady charmer takes off his 'date face' and looks at self

I've been getting to know attractive single men who yearn for a long-term relationship. Where were these guys when I was single and in the market? I never saw them. Yet now that I am happily married and writing this column, I find men whom most would consider to be great catches. Each guy tells me he is eager to be in a serious relationship but can't find one.

I know the woman's side of this story. I was curious about the man's. So I sat down with one such friend, Rick, to hear his story. He said it was unusual for him to talk about his relationships. Most of his buddies don't. But Rick was eager for a sympathetic ear and he had given a lot of thought to his personal life.

Just six weeks earlier, Rick had lost his latest girlfriend. He was heartbroken. "She was the most wonderful woman, but I didn't appreciate what we had," he says with remorse. "I took her for granted and became complacent about the relationship."

It was the third relationship in six years that ended this way and Rick was seeing a pattern.

Rick told me he goes through three distinct phases.

Phase One lasts about six months. Rick loves the challenge of meeting women and does so with ease. He may collect six or seven phone numbers in a month. "Getting those numbers is validation in itself," he says.

He puts on his "date face." At age thirty-seven, he is fit and trim. Well-employed, he drives a white convertible and has a pilot's license. He's smooth on the dance floor. He buys dinner. He says and does the right things to impress women. He's effective.

"I get what I want: validation from a female," he says. "Being seen with a physically and socially attractive mate boosts my ego. I have a guaranteed date for every Saturday night. I've got someone I can bring home to mom. I prefer to have a girlfriend (rather) than to be single. When I'm accepted by a beautiful woman, *I'm in*. It's like wearing a badge of honor. If a little hottie is interested in me, it tells everyone that I qualify. Lonely single guys don't get validation like that."

Phase Two lasts about ten months. Rick told me that after he's got the woman "hook, line and sinker" and the relationship has become set in stone, he starts to reveal another side of his personality and the woman gets disillusioned.

"I know I have her. I don't abuse her in any way, but we stop doing exciting things like going out on the town." There are no more trips to the river, no more picnics in the countryside, no more long talks in coffee houses.

Rick said that his girlfriends remained consistently attractive and appealing, but it was he who had changed. Dinner and dancing were replaced by trips to Blockbuster. He put on weight and spent most of his time on the couch eating chips and fondling the remote control. Work and concern over his aging father stressed him to the point that his mind was no longer on the relationship. He'd sneak cigarettes. She felt neglected. She had been leading an active, healthy life and didn't want to be brought down by him. He knew that he failed to live up to her standards.

"I got pudgy and smelled like an ashtray," he says. "I would have broken up with me, too."

Why did he let that happen? Rick told me that, knowing they were exclusive with each other, he felt that they had already crossed the finish line and so didn't have to keep up the pace. "Once the deer is strung up in the barn, the hunt is over," he said.

Rick initiated his roles in phases One and Two, but Phase Three was always forced on him. The girlfriend pulled away and Rick tried unsuccessfully to salvage the relationship. Flowers and promises to change weren't enough to win her back.

Nothing registered with Rick when two previous girlfriends got married after they dumped him. But the recent breakup hurt so much that Rick wanted to analyze what he had done to cause it. He wanted to figure out how to change that behavior.

While nursing a broken heart, he went on a diet and started to run, bike and swim. He updated his wardrobe. He took stock of himself and started all over.

Learning to be comfortable with himself is Rick's greatest challenge. "Loneliness is a bear," he says. "I don't mind being by myself now, but I don't want to be single when I'm in my fifties. In order to avoid Phase Three, I need to modify my behavior in phases One and Two. Next time I won't hit the throttle so hard in Phase One. That just builds expectations that are difficult to fulfill long-term. I think I should refrain from getting involved so quickly. It's hard for me to be comfortable on my own, but it is important that I be able do that. It requires a conscious decision to be in a relationship. Now I realize how I must always demonstrate my appreciation to my partner when she's made that choice."

He adds, "I'm curious about how unique my situation is."

As I spoke with Rick, I learned that he constantly compares himself against others. When a stranger passes, Rick always measures how he ranks and says to himself, "I have him beat." That kind of competitiveness is bred into American males starting with Little League. Rick thinks he has most guys beat on the physical, material level. But they may have the edge when it comes to self-confidence and inner peace. By his own admission, he doesn't have too much in that department.

"If I see someone who has me beat, it hits a nerve. But I reassure myself that I'm still in the top fifteen percentile."

"Todd" (detail) 4" x 7" x 8," ceramic, acrylic, wax, 2002

34

Better loving through technology, robots for your personal pleasure

Modern technology has enhanced our lives in oh so many ways, but what can it do for your love life? More than you might realize.

Much has been written about the dark side of sex and the Internet. With headlines about lurking pedophiles, on-line infidelity and addiction to adult sites, we might fail to appreciate the good things about techno-sex.

The Internet, digital cameras and wireless devices enable pervasive communication that transcends geographic boundaries, and on-line social networks provide ever widening ways to meet.

Technologies such as e-mail, chat rooms, instant messaging and mobile devices are deployed by those looking for love. According to comScore, more than twenty million Internet users in the United States visited on-line dating sites like match.com and eHarmony in December 2006. And the U.S. on-line dating market will reach more than nine hundred million dollars in 2011, according to JupiterResearch.

I claim a small but important role in the birth of the on-line dating phenomenon. In 1988, while working for Prodigy, I conceived of and managed the first consumer-based on-line bulletin board where subscribers could specifically discuss romance and relationships. We discovered that people find it easier to be honest when writing e-mail or text than talking face-to-face. One couple met on-line and married in six months.

With free services such as skype.com, it's easy to track when friends are on-line. You can exchange instant messages, talk and even see them as they talk to you—or as they do anything in front of their webcam. A lure of on-line flirtation once was that you could hide behind the technology ("On the Internet, no one knows you're a dog"), but now video phones add visuals. Many physical clues, from body language to odd twitches, were missing from on-line dating services, instant messages and still images, but now are communicated in real time and make a cyber-date truly possible.

For some nervous soul-mate seekers, technology has been liberating. Virtual dating (in chat rooms or in on-line communities like SecondLife.com) eliminates the safety concerns that prevent many people from meeting in person.

One need not go on-line unchaperoned. Engage.com, for example, allows members to bring with them on-line friends and family, all of whom can prowl the profiles, checking people out and matching them up. Members can also rate the politeness of their dates, as well as the accuracy of the profiles. This new "community" approach to on-line matching is also evident in sprawling new social networking sites such as Facebook, Friendster and MySpace. MySpace alone has more than a hundred million members. Although these social networking sites appeal mainly to young users and are not strictly dating sites, they bring community back into whatever dating is generated there. And several on-line services are now built entirely around claims that they have powerful, effective, scientific matchmaking tests.

Would-be suitors can find all kinds of support on-line. Girl-friendx.com helps fellows remember key dates, events and the little things—scroll through a list of pre-written "sweet things to say" and even select an entire series of prepared text messages and schedule them in advance. Then, no matter what he's really up to, she'll think that he's only thinking of her. He can also set up his own phone to call himself with an "emergency" to bail him out of a bad date.

Gals can get recommendations from other women about good guys at GreatBoyfriends.com, but they should probably cross-reference him first on DontDateHimGirl.com.

Digital cameras are used for both personal and commercial porn. One great advantage of a phone camera is that no nosy film developer gets to look at the pictures you take.

Why does porn play such a key role in driving the mass adoption of new technologies? Sex sells. Sex sells particularly well to almost the same demographic as new technology: young men.

Populations obviously wouldn't grow without sex; many technologies wouldn't either. What was most played on video cassette recorders when they came on the market? Porno movies. What major social change came about with the launch of the automobile? Youngsters would borrow the family car so they could make out with privacy (and many still do so today). These inventions were not created with sexuality in mind, but that didn't stop such use of them.

A steamy spot where technology and sex converge is called "teledildonics." Dildonics are sex toys that can be controlled by a computer. Teledildonics (also known as cyberdildonics) is the integration of telepresence with sex. (The term was coined in the nineteen-eighties by Ted Nelson.)

Currently, the computer-human interfaces are crude, but soon you'll be able to program your dildo to vibrate or gyrate in sync with movies on your favorite porn site or to the music on your iPod.

Sue Johanson of the Canadian cable television show, *Talk Sex with Sue,* reported on a survey: "I'm delighted to find that about a third of the thirteen-thousand five hundred respondents said that sex-tech has helped their love lives, versus only seven percent who feel it has harmed them. Also, men and women responded to this question pretty much the same—no huge disconnects here."

35

Improve your love relationships by using the Law of Attraction

The Law of Attraction says that all forms of matter and energy are attracted to that which is of a like vibration. You are a living magnet. You get what you put your energy into and focus on, whether wanted or unwanted. Whether you are aware of it or not, every thought you have, every emotion you feel, everything you hear and read, affects your reality. Once you are aware of this law and how it works, you can start to use it to deliberately attract into your life what you want.

I was introduced to this concept about a year ago, when I read *Ask and It Is Given: Learning to Manifest Your Desires*, by Esther and Jerry Hicks. The Texas-based authors claim that the material in their book was channeled by a collection of disembodied spirits known collectively as Abraham. In spite of my considerable skepticism about its origin, I read the book and was surprised by how much of it rang true. I recognized truths about life and relationships that I had known but had forgotten. Then I read another book that I've come to love, *Excuse Me, Your Life Is Waiting: The Astonishing Power of Feelings*, by Lynn

Grabhorn. With nonstop humor and in a down-to-earth practical manner, she explains what she learned from the Hickses.

For centuries there have been proponents of the Law of Attraction, but it was recently popularized in the documentary *The Secret*, after Oprah devoted an entire show to it.

While *The Secret* focuses on gaining material wealth, the Law of Attraction is said to work equally well with love.

I think that is what was at play when I met my husband. For years I had thought I was ready to find a life partner, but no relationship stuck. I got to the point where I no longer really expected to meet Mr. Right. I remember one night some sixteen years ago, talking to girlfriends and affirming, in a way that felt different from in the past, that I *really felt ready* for a good relationship. That week he showed up at my house with a couple I had invited.

The Law of Attraction teaches that as you ask for the kind of relationship you want, visualize it, believe in it and feel good about it persistently, the universe is arranging for an appropriate person to come into your life in the fastest, quickest and most harmonious way, without hindering the other's freedom.

Wouldn't it be nice if it were always just so simple—that merely thinking of something or someone would manifest the subject of your heart's desire? These days it doesn't *usually* work that way for me. And I imagine that there are an untold number of lonely single people who would also say that it doesn't work for them. They think a lot about having a good relationship, but wind up with no one or the wrong one. I'm still married, but there are still plenty of days when nothing I want seems to come my way.

I remind myself that if I create my own reality, I can't blame anyone else for what my life is like.

To quote Lynn Grabhorn, "If we are verbally or mentally accusing, berating or disapproving in any way, we are attracting negatively.

"If we are feeling trapped, ignored or neglected, unsafe, misunderstood or shortchanged we are attracting negatively."

That's focusing on *what we don't want*. We are equipped with built-in meters so we can tell if we are attracting what we like or don't like. According to Hicks, when we feel predominately positive, then we are predominately in harmony with our desires. Any slight feeling of negativity, even ennui, lethargy or resignation, is our signal that, if we keep thinking the thoughts we're presently thinking, we'll create something out of harmony with what we really want. Grabhorn postulates that calamities that beset innocent victims, like wars and tsunamis, are the result of collective negative thought patterns.

We may know better than to succumb to negativity after seeing *The Secret*, but it is hard to open up our feel-good valves and to keep them open if we are disgusted by what's around us. And it's *impossible* when *we* don't believe that it's possible that we will get what we want. Old habits and belief systems are hard to change, but it is doable, and there's plenty of incentive to try.

Think about how much improved your sexual response will be when, instead of carrying a chip on your shoulder, you crank up your vibration level to the point where you feel truly happy about being with someone and appreciative of your lover's qualities, warts and all.

Are the concepts presented in *The Secret* true? Does the Law of Attraction rule everything? That question is like "Is there a God?" I rather favor believing in it. It feels better than to not.

When you are truly keeping your feel-good valves open, there is a sense of free flow. Things start to happen. If you are open to having a loving relationship in your life, you may meet someone. You may even fall in love. Trusting this process feels like being swept away by a gentle, yet exhilarating stream. You feel drawn where you want to go, to people who nourish and enrich your life. It's an experience not unlike orgasm, a peak experience.

More and more people I meet are believers, too. We're all working on feeling good, getting clear, attracting ideal partners, experiencing abundance and finding peace. At some point, we hope, a critical mass of consciousness will transform the world.

36

Why do people want to have sex?
For reasons varied and complex

I didn't really feel like having sex the other day, but I did it anyway. My motivation wasn't very clear. I had some free time. There was an opportunity to join my husband while he was taking a siesta. I assumed correctly that he'd welcome my initiative, and I said to myself, "Why not?" I thought that it would relax me and help me get out of my head. It did.

The reasons we choose to have sex vary from person to person and from time to time. People do it for serious life-affirming reasons, for frivolous debauchery and everything in between.

"Historically, the reasons people have sex have been assumed to be few in number and simple in nature—to reproduce, to experience pleasure or to relieve sexual tension." So wrote a couple of professors from the University of Texas at Austin. Cindy Meston and David Buss, both PhDs in the Department of Psychology, have published a thorough taxonomy of sexual motivation in the Archives of Sexual Behavior after conducting a scientific study of why people have sex—an extremely important, but surprisingly little-studied topic.

Research in the nineteen-seventies, -eighties and -nineties showed that people had sex for many other reasons that were varied and psychologically complex. These included a desire for pure pleasure, to express emotional closeness, to please a partner and to make a conquest. Yet most of the reasons documented in those decades implicitly assumed the context of an ongoing romantic relationship or long-term mateship. Humans, however, have a menu of mating strategies, including long-term, short-term and extra curricular mating. There might be reasons for having sex with a casual partner such as the desire to experience sexual variety or seeking to improve one's sexual skills. Sex could be exchanged for favors, special privileges, a preferred job or indeed for any resource.

Sex might be used to reward a partner or as a favor in exchange for something the partner has done. Or sex might be used to retaliate against a partner for some perceived wrongdoing. Also, sex might be used to intensify the relationship, escalate the level of commitment within the relationship or turn a relationship from short- to long-term. Women, in particular, were thought to engage in sexual intercourse for emotional closeness, bonding, commitment, love, affection, acceptance, tolerance and closeness.

In their recent study, Meston and Buss surveyed more than four hundred men and women ranging in age from seventeen years to fifty-two years, who responded to the query: "Please list all the reasons you can think of why you, or someone you have known, has engaged in sexual intercourse in the past." The more than seven hundred answers collected resulted in two hundred thirty-seven distinct reasons.

After they had compiled that long list, Meston and Buss asked more than fifteen hundred college students, in exchange for psychology class credits, to rank the reasons in terms of how they applied to their experiences. Keep in mind that these results reveal the behavior of those who are of an age when, Meston conceded, "Hormones run rampant." She predicted significant differences when older people are studied.

The research found similar reasons for why these young adults got intimate, and the Number One reason was simply: "I was attracted to the person." While the primary reason involved lust, rather than amour, expressing love and showing affection still were in the top ten for both men and women.

Gender differences were negligible. Twenty of the top twenty-five reasons given were the same for males and females. "Men were more likely to be opportunistic towards having sex," Meston said. "So, if sex was...available, they would jump on it—somewhat more so than women. Women were more likely to have sex because they felt they needed to please their partner." Men, the study revealed, were more apt than women to have sex to get things like a promotion, a raise or a favor. Guys were much more likely than gals to say they'd had sex to "boost my social status" or because the partner was famous or "out of my league."

The study Meston and Buss completed inspired *New York Times* science writer John Tierney to provide an on-line forum where the public could add their ideas to the list of reasons to have sex. In just a few days he got hundreds of responses, which prompted the UT researchers to add forty reasons to their list.

Reading the many tawdry reasons why others have sex, I felt more inclined to forgive my own past foibles.

The reasons I found scariest involved revenge: "I wanted to give someone else a sexually transmitted disease (e.g., herpes, AIDS)," "I wanted to get rid of aggression" and "I thought it would help 'trap' a new partner."

The most inspiring reasons involved celebration: "Because life is short (and a hundred years from now we will all be dust)," "To recover or reaffirm life after the loss of (a) loved one" and "I wanted to become one with another person."

While we may wish to keep the rationalizations for our behavior to ourselves, the act of reasoning itself has value. By delving into our own feelings and getting honest with ourselves about why we get it on, we'll gain greater personal understanding of and appreciation for our own sexual natures.

"Embracing Couple" (detail) 9" x 13.5" x 24," bronze, 2003

*I*ndex of Illustrations

About the Artist

The illustrations in this book are images of bronze and ceramic sculpture created by my husband, Arye Shapiro. Some of them are in private collections and some are available for sale.

When I was single, I thought that I wanted to marry an artist. My father, a physician, wanted me to marry a doctor or a scientist. When I met Arye in 1992, he was a scientist with a PhD in physics from the University of Arizona. We married—and he turned into an artist!

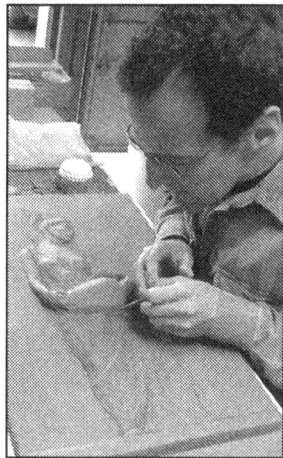

Arye Shapiro

In 1998 Arye was working in the semiconductor industry developing the next generation of computer chips. During that year he enrolled in a figurative sculpture class and discovered his passion, his talent and his lifework. He has since sculpted numerous commissions for private clients and the Catholic Church.

Arye studied figure sculpture at the Austin Sculpture Center and the Loveland Academy of Fine Arts in Colorado and has been influenced by art in the great museums and cathedrals of Europe. He taught sculpture classes at the Austin Sculpture Center and the Sculpture Academy of Austin.

Arye works with professional models and makes sculptures of clients. Arye often works on the same pose for one or two months. Sometimes he'll draw or photograph a model from several angles and use the drawings and images as reference.

When working on a commissioned sculpture, Arye interviews the clients to fully understand the context of their subject and their intentions for displaying the artwork. Clients review and approve the selection of the pose, the maquette (a rough sketch in clay), the completed clay sculpture prior to firing or casting and the final patina.

For commissioned portrait sculpture, Arye will take as many as a hundred digital photographs of clients. If desired, he will work from their favorite historical photos or home videos.

Ceramic figures are first modeled in water-based clay. The clay is kept moist over a period of weeks while the form is refined. After Arye has finished modeling a clay sculpture, it is allowed to dry for one to two months before being slowly fired to about 1915° Fahrenheit in an electric kiln.

To achieve the final color in ceramic sculpture, Arye applies a faux patina consisting of several layers of dilute acrylic paint, followed by two thin layers of colored wax. The piece is buffed to the desired sheen.

If Arye plans to create a sculpture in bronze, the original piece is modeled in plastilina (oil-based clay). An exact bronze replica is cast at a local foundry using the lost wax process. Since this process involves creation of a high-fidelity rubber mold, it is possible to cast multiple bronze copies (a limited edition) of the original sculpture.

Color images of the work seen in this book are available upon request. Also, additional images of Arye's sculpture can be seen at his web site: www.figure-sculpture.com.

Arye can turn your idea into sculpture. You may contact him via e-mail at arye@figure-sculpture.com.

More Intimacies

If you enjoyed reading this collection and would like more,
there's plenty to anticipate. Look for a second volume of
original columns and additional artwork,
coming soon.

Please visit
www.TrueIntimacies.com